"This book is frustrating. It's frustrating k
nature's quest for power. It's frustrating b
wisdom's preservation of status quo. Mostly, it's frustrating because it's so
biblical and Christ-centered that there's no way for a follower of Jesus to
dismiss it. Caveat Lector: Let the Reader Beware! This will not be easy to
absorb, but it is necessary if we ever hope to become the beloved community imagined in Scripture."

—**John Alan Turner**, Church Consultant, Author of *Crazy Stories; Sane God*

"We modern evangelicals have long been proponents of 'defending the
faith,' but rarely have we stopped to ask 'Defending if from what or (maybe
more appropriately) whom?' and when the faith has been adequately defended, 'Who was defeated in the process?' Sean invites us into a better
story, an unapologetically biblical story that has been there all along. It's not
about acquiescing to culture, it's about the way of Christ, which is laying
down our lives for those around us."

—**Shane Blackshear**, Writer and host of the podcasts Seminary Dropout
and OnRamp

Unarmed Empire

UNARMED
EMPIRE

IN SEARCH
OF BELOVED
COMMUNITY

Sean Palmer

FOREWORD BY
Scot McKnight

 CASCADE *Books* • Eugene, Oregon

UNARMED EMPIRE
In Search of Beloved Community

Cascade Books
An Imprint of Wipf and Stock Publishers
199 W. 8th Ave., Suite 3
Eugene, OR 97401

www.wipfandstock.com

PAPERBACK ISBN: 978-1-4982-9070-8
HARDCOVER ISBN: 978-1-4982-9072-2
EBOOK ISBN: 978-1-4982-9071-5

Cataloguing-in-Publication data:

Names: Palmer, Sean, author. | McKnight, Scot, foreword.

Title: Unarmed empire : in search of beloved community / Sean Palmer ; foreword by Scot McKnight.

Description: Eugene, OR: Cascade Books, 2017 | Includes bibliographical references.

Identifiers: ISBN 978-1-4982-9070-8 (paperback) | ISBN 978-1-4982-9072-2 (hardcover) | ISBN 978-1-4982-9071-5 (ebook)

Subjects: LCSH: Nonviolence—Religious aspects—Christianity.

Classification: BT736.6 .P35 2017 (print) | BT736.6 .P35 (ebook)

Manufactured in the U.S.A.   10/19/17

Malia and Katharine,

For showing me it's possible to
smile with your whole life.

I am sending you out armed with vulnerability, like lambs
walking into a pack of wolves.

—Jesus, Luke 10:3

I believe that unarmed truth and unconditional love will
have the final word in reality.

—Martin Luther King Jr.

Contents

Foreword

SEAN PALMER IS A storyteller—a Southern storyteller if you want to know the precise genre. He's also a preacher who loves the Bible. I'd like to say he's a born storyteller and preacher and Bible guy, but that's not quite right. One has to learn these arts, but I am willing to say that these arts run deeper than his baptism, and that's saying a lot for someone whose identity is a Churches of Christ preacher. That he's black reshapes each of these arts, but you will have to read *Unarmed Empire* to see how that reshaping works. Once you read it you will not only see this reshaping, but you will rise up with me and call him (and us) blessed, even doubly blessed.

Sean Palmer is a pastor, and the way the church acts—the way it despises the Other; the way it speaks of those unlike them; the way politics run deeper than Jesus; the way Americanism and nationalism and empire ideologies strike the chord that moves them, and so on—bothers him enough to do two things. First, he names the sins of the church and sometimes its perpetrators. Second, he names a way forward—not a way around and not a way under—but a way out of the chaos into the order of God's kingdom, where we see Jesus gathering around him folks who want to follow him by loving all.

Most importantly, Sean Palmer is a witness—to Jesus, to the church, to the kingdom, to honesty (about himself), to grace, to change, and to a courageous vision in the midst of empire. Here are some themes of Sean's witness:

First, he is a witness to an unarmed empire, which in his language is about peace and about the church being lambs among wolves. He will point his finger at some brutal immoralities, but he points even more to the way—excuse me—to The Way who is the truth and the life. An unarmed empire is a beautiful expression and most of us will love the turn of phrase, but once we get his point we'd perhaps not like to have heard it.

Why? Because "unarmed empire" is a summons to live as God revealed himself in Christ. That means we have to drop our swords, and we have lots of metaphorical ones.

Second, Sean has a way of getting under my skin as he was searching for my heart. Jesus was an amazing storyteller, and one of his best stories was about the Pharisee and the tax collector. Many of us read it with a bit of delight, if not Schadenfreude, for we love watching Jesus squash the Pharisee and raise up the tax collector. We approve of Jesus excoriating the Pharisee because we take delight in knowing that we are not the Pharisee—but the moment that happens, we have become the Pharisee. How so? We sit in judgment on him as he sat in judgment on the tax collector. Sean tells stories in the same manner, and he intentionally gets under our skin and makes us nervous about where he might end up this time, only for us to realize he's not nit picking or irritating us on purpose. He's trying to get to our heart and to get us to see the heart of Jesus. He does this well.

Finally, some people tell their story in such a way that you want to meet them. We Google their name and we find more books by them and about them on Amazon or in the library, and we make them heroes. I receive books like this weekly. But there's something more in Sean's witness: he tells stories in such a way that I want to meet his God. I want to encounter his Jesus. I want to read his Bible. In other words, his stories are tools to get us to see that what God is doing in this world is bigger than who we are. It is a story of grace that summons us to put down our swords and guns and fight for an unarmed king in an unarmed kingdom.

It's enough that many may well want to go back to church.

—Scot McKnight

Acknowledgments

THIS BOOK IS THE result of a lifetime in the church. Its heart and purpose is the praise of the church that raised me (even as I critique and ask her tough questions), to press contemporary churches to become more like what Jesus and the New Testament envision, and to paint a more alluring portrait of what the Christian church can become. Accordingly, its production is the fruit of the church—both the church gathered and scattered. I want to thank The Vine Church in Temple, Texas, for their generosity toward the Kingdom for allowing me the time and space to make this book a reality. There is, in my opinion, no church on earth like The Vine. Along with The Vine, I am indebted to all the churches in which I've worshipped and served, and now Ecclesia Houston. I have been made better by knowing and loving you.

Special thanks to my mother-in-law, Beverly Stripling Strack, for not only raising a fabulously thoughtful and beautiful daughter, but also for being the first person to read the entire manuscript and for lending her proofreading skills.

Also much thanks to my friends, Jordan Hubbard, Jeremy Houck, Dr. Shaun Burrow, Chad Higgins, Dr. Kraig Martin, Jeff Brooks, and countless men and women who served as reflection points and encouragers throughout this project. Jonathan Storment is due special attention for being the person who gave me a call one afternoon and said, "You really should write a book." He had a vision (and belief) for this work long before anyone else. In much the same way, John Alan Turner deserves much credit for his insight into the book-writing process and his partnership in multiple writing processes, as well as our podcast *Not So Black and White with Sean Palmer and John Alan Turner*. I trust John's instincts and love for God's church.

Gloria Palmer, my mother, has been the most devoted follower of my life and work. Mom made a simple rule when I was a kid: You will go to church until you're 18, then you can choose for yourself. She made life alongside and inside God's community a priority and it stuck. Her steady, unswerving dedication to my spiritual formation has been, and continues to be, a rock to which I return. This book is the result of her prayers.

After knowing one another for most of our lives, thank you Rochelle, my bride, for still believing I have something to say. Whatever is good here is because of your tireless efforts, drawing me toward my better angels. You are God's greatest earthly gift to me. I cannot imagine a world without you in it. I wouldn't want that world if it did exist.

Introduction

It's a thing to see when a boy comes home.

—John Steinbeck, *The Grapes of Wrath*

I F I WERE BETTER at property management, my former church would have had much more curb appeal. Often the grass on the back lawn grew too long before whomever was supposed to mow it got around to mowing it, or whoever was supposed to call the guy who was supposed to mow it called the guy. A stronger leader would have had an efficient process. I didn't.

Another exhibition of my managerial failure was our church parking lot. The pavement was—and I imagine, still is—ruptured and torn apart from age and disinterest. In fact, there are sections at the rear of the lot that, unless you're driving Big Foot, you wouldn't want to drive across. There it sits, cracked and chewed up gravel and rocky pieces of black and white concrete upended by wear and tear and, oh yeah, those trucks almost as big as Big Foot (it's Texas).

Our fragmented parking lot remained disintegrated on purpose, though. Each year the unattended rubble at the rear of that property hosts multiple families of killdeer, which are shorebirds who don't always live by the shore. In fact, they love parking lots. Mother killdeer are brown on the back with black and white stripes around their necks. Parking lots make great camouflage. Every spring they would lay eggs in the wrecked rock of our mangled parking lot. Killdeer eggs are speckled, black and white. In the ruins of the parking lot, their eggs were nearly undetectable.

Our church kids would shriek with excitement each spring when the momma killdeer lay their eggs; drivers make sure to avoid their habitat.

Their presence on our property even stumbled its way into casual conversations: "Be mindful of the killdeer eggs." These weren't just *any* killdeer, they were *our* killdeer.

John runs the church soundboard. John is gracious, but is also a no nonsense, plain spoken saint who wasn't born in a pew. Each week, before our band kicks on the loud speakers, John can be found around the side of the church building grabbing the last drag off his pre-worship cigarette.

After visiting the killdeer with my nine-year-old daughter one Sunday morning, I spotted John headed toward their cracked interim incubator. This time, instead of clutching his cigarette between his index and middle fingers, John carried a pair of orange highway cones. He was headed toward the killdeer. John plopped the cones on both sides of the squawking, terrorized momma killdeer and just walked away. She didn't know John's intentions, but John and the momma killdeer were partners in protecting her babies from soon-to-be arriving cars and trucks, threats we knew were coming, but she couldn't imagine. Our church knew the killdeer eggs were there. Our visitors didn't. The momma killdeer needed a little help from our church for her eggs to stay safe. She just didn't know it.

Killdeer are not rare birds. There's no Washington lobby dedicated to their conservation. There are no zoos hosting elaborate festivities to educate the public. Killdeer are common. I suspect some folks wouldn't think twice about the death of a few killdeer eggs, especially if they were crushed under tire by accident. Not that church.

Our congregation wasn't a bunch of hippies, and we didn't pass out literature from The Sierra Club. If it's in our power, we simply loved and protected whatever needed love and protection. If we could safeguard others against harm, why not? We couldn't fix everything in the world, but we could touch everything in our little world in small town Texas.

Even more than killdeer and eggs, we loved and protected people who were vulnerable, especially those who had wandered away from God and church. John and his orange cones are emblematic of what we believe every church—every Christian—should be: walking, talking dispensers of acceptance, welcome, and, yes, protection. God's vision for the church (the people of God) is a hospitable people who are open, embracing, and protective of all people all the time. That's what it means to be the church.

Unfortunately, "church" has become a bad word. The reasons are simple. When I talk with non-Christians about "church," they talk about political speeches disguised as "sermons" and happy-clappy, poorly orchestrated, fantasy-laden, alternative-reality "worship" music. My unchurched friends equate "church" with boldfaced hypocrisy and national "Christian" spokespersons who claim Jesus but have never adopted his speech ethics or social priorities.

These are certainly a caricature of the church, but they are real and problematic perceptions. Popular notions about church are to blame for sure, but the church itself isn't without liability. Like a character on a reality TV show, the video displays events that actually happened. The character and characters we display, regardless of editing, only show what we give them to show. If we don't like what we see on the film, we can only fault ourselves for giving them the footage.

The New Testament offers a more alluring picture of what church means and what she is designed to do. In particular, the letters of the Apostle Paul compose a portrait of a church that embraces people of different races, politics, economics, gender, and worldviews. Through the mechanism of the church, Paul confronts sex, sexuality, gender roles, ethnocentrism, politics, and poverty. As crazy as it sounds, Paul believes the church of Jesus is broad, bold, and grace-filled enough to house divergent people under the banner of Christ and deploy them to love the world as God loves. The church is intended to be the best kind of home—a place of welcome and hospitality for *all* people.

My hope is to convince you that the elixir you have been looking for—the cure for social marginalization, for the migration of the "Nones" away from churches, for the increasing scorn some Christians feel in the public square, and the divided and hostile political discourse engaged in by cultural Christians—is found in the kind of church Paul's letters intended to create and shape. New strategies, better programs, skinny jeans, louder music, and hipster beards won't rescue the church from the sticky position we now find ourselves in. We need a new imagination. An imagination that understands what Paul means by "new creation." Through story and scripture, I hope to convince you that the task of becoming the humble and hospitable church is the job of the people of God, not only professors, theologians, and pastors.

I hope to paint a picture that stirs your heart for God and love for our sisters and brothers and for the marginalized and Other. I hope to convince you that the church of Jesus was intended to be the place you've always been looking for. Every story I've shared is true, but true in the sense that I've recounted them as I remember them and as my journals and previous writings reflect them. For ease, some of the people you'll meet are two people, sometimes three, who shared core characteristics, virtues, and sometime vices. Instead of more people to know, I've chosen to give you fewer. Like *Dragnet*, some of the names, places, and locations have been changed. Unlike *Dragnet*, these adaptations are not to protect the innocent, but to protect the guilty. I've done nothing to protect my own guilt, however. This work is about welcome and hospitality and how the church of Jesus is that place and in reality is the only place that can ever be that place. I believe, down to my marrow, that embrace rather than exclusion is what God intended when God birthed the community who carries God's name.

In a culture of religious suspicion, the time of cultural Christianity and the illusion that Christians and churches should enjoy a seat at the table and a privileged hearing in the halls of power has passed. Now we are faced with—and can enjoy—new opportunities to inhabit a very old story. Perhaps the cozy way America's Christian-dominate culture existed without question, pushback, and accountability, conspired to create lazy churches which could comfortably co-exist in and oversee the morays of society without the burden of dealing with her own failings.

The age of Christendom has failed the gospel in some significant ways. It allowed us to use the name "Christian" without being disciples of Christ.

Why bother, for instance, dealing with racial injustice as long as churches were filled on Sundays and Christian celebrities remained welcomed in City Hall, on Capital Hill, and in The White House? Why fool around with gender equity when the majority culture largely agreed—with little resistance—that families, communities, and nations were better off when women stayed home and cooked and mopped wearing diamond earrings and pearl necklaces. There was a time when the church needn't ask the questions ripping at her seams today. Christian churches have enjoyed so much privilege they have lost sight of their purpose. Perhaps in our loss of privilege we will once again find our purpose and become God's community of healing and reconciliation. We've ceased—in many ways—to be a manifestation of the eternal Kingdom of God lived in a local community. We lost what it means to reflect justice, reconciliation, peace, love, and wisdom in ways, and by means, that nothing else in the world can or does.

Come Home

A few years ago, I saw singer-songwriter Jason Mraz on *VH1 Storytellers*. On *Storytellers* artists share the stories behind their most popular songs. The first song of the night was "93 Million Miles." In the final line of the chorus Mraz sings, "Just know, you're never alone, you can always come back home."

Mraz travels the world touring so he rarely lays his head in the same place two nights in a row. For him "home" is a state of mind. It's who you are, wherever you are, and the hospitality given and received by the people you're with. The night I saw Mraz was four months before Easter. When I heard "93 Million Miles," I knew it was the perfect sentiment for our Easter. What Jason Mraz was really talking about was church. He just didn't know it. He was singing about a place anyone, anywhere can belong to; a place anyone, anywhere can come back to without judgment; a place of welcome and acceptance.

Church is a unique community in the world, but most folks don't think it's worth much. Church has become just another place for insiders and outsiders, another club with privileges and exclusions, another means to broker power and leverage control. Believers, as well as those antagonistic to faith, have legitimized this popular, but damaging notion. As we do so, we're cheating meaning from our lives by choosing a thoughtless and effortless path.

Looking at the arc of my life, I see that whatever positive seeds of character God deposited within me were watered and nurtured in Christian community. The same is true of the people whom I most admire and the public figures I've come to most fully commend. Through the church I learned about hospitality to strangers, peacemaking, loving and praying for my enemies, and the active formation and practice of the fruit of the Spirit. Christianity is a kind of performance art. The muscles of faith are chiseled in the presence of other believers. We are nurtured in the ways of grace, not by books, podcasts, worship concerts or conferences, but by the church herself. We are guided along the path by fellow travelers. Even though history is littered with men and women who tried to circumnavigate faith solo, the best practitioners of faith always did so in community and managed to heal their tiny parcel of God's creation as part of the project.

Real People + Real God + Real Life = Real Church

Real churches are a home for everyone, always. I was reminded of that recently when I recalled an odd story I read in college about a young girl who got lost in her town. The city where the girl lived wasn't big enough to be dangerous in the same way really large cities can be. It was big enough that being lost was a problem.

The girl, distressed as she was, somehow stumbled upon a police officer that asked her if she needed help. "Yes." Since she couldn't remember her home phone number or street address, the officer decided to drive her to the police station, asking her if she spotted anything that looked familiar along the way. She didn't . . . until she did!

What she spotted was her church.

Ecstatic, she shouted, "Pull over there! That's my church. It's basically my home."

I hope that is what reading these pages does for you. Maybe it will for your son, daughter, or grandchildren. Maybe together local Christian churches can become the places our mothers or fathers, aunts, uncles, cousins, friends, neighbors, coworkers, teachers, students or whomever can find and call home. I hope it reminds us all that the church should be home—the place we are both challenged and accepted, sanctified and loved just as we are while showing us what to become.

Maybe we can find our way home to what Jesus intended. Maybe we can find our way home to one another. Maybe we can find our way home alongside strangers and people who aren't like us. Perhaps we can help our friends and neighbors who have come to expect church to feel like the coldest place on earth to experience it as the warmest place on earth. Maybe you'll see that church is all the things you always wanted it to be—humble, loving, accepting, and healing.

Church should feel like coming home. It doesn't for everyone. That reality must change. Maybe by the time you lay down these words, after we've walked together for a while, and wrestled with all the hope, beauty, and struggles facing God's children both inside and outside the church, we can figure out how to make the church a home for everyone.

If my church parking lot can become home for killdeer, what might those small birds reveal to us about our greater capacity to become a home for anyone?

A few months after our killdeer nested, their chicks were born and the killdeer moved on. It wasn't long after that when the playground at the rear of our church property welcomed a new life form: rabbits. We had rabbits everywhere. It's like they were being born, you know, like rabbits. My youngest daughter, Katharine, is nine and loves to come to church early with me on Sundays. After weeks of seeing more and more rabbits invade our space, she said something I'll never forget. She asked, "Look at all these rabbits, Daddy. Where did they come from?" Then, with her childlike purity she asked, "Do you think the birds told them this was a safe place?"

"I hope so Katharine."

I hope my church, your church, and all churches can be a safe place. This is what it means to live in an unarmed empire.

1

Burn a Church

If you love god, burn a church.

—Jello Biafra, lead singer, Dead Kennedys

THE TRIANGLE SHIRTWAIST FACTORY specialized in manufacturing women's garments. By today's standards, it would be called a sweatshop, the kind of space you might expect to find tucked away in a remote niche of the world. But the Triangle Shirtwaist Factory wasn't located in some remote outpost. The factory was a mainstay in New York City. The majority of the employees were immigrants, mostly German and Eastern European, and most of those immigrants were women, girls really. Workers, some as young as twelve years old, labored through fourteen-hour shifts for the whopping total of $7 per week.

On March 25, 1911, the Triangle Shirtwaist Factory caught fire. These were the days before any real workplace or safety regulations. Companies were largely allowed to treat their employees any way they saw fit. The floors of the Triangle Shirtwaist Factory were littered with scraps of fabric, debris, and flammable textiles were tightly crammed into storage closets. Employees and managers smoked and discarded their cigarette butts onto the floor. Water buckets were placed around the factory floor to extinguish small fires, which were common.

Walking into any business this afternoon you might see a sign: *This door to remain unlocked during business hours.* One reason those signs exist is the Triangle Shirtwaist Factory. In 1911, the doors—in accordance with store policy—were locked.

It was theft prevention. The owners of the Triangle Shirtwaist Factory were making sure their young, poor factory workers weren't stealing fabric. They wanted to guarantee the makers weren't takers. At the end of each day, the girls exited single file, out the few unlocked passageways.

At 4:45 that afternoon, someone on the eighth floor of the factory yelled, "Fire!" It was during a shift change while the girls were putting on their coats to leave. Someone grabbed a pail of water, but it was too late. The fire was already raging. Matters got worse. Overpopulated factory floors, combined with locked doors, forced employees to jam themselves into el-evators and narrow fire escapes.

The fire spread from the eighth to the ninth and tenth floors. Sixty-nine women made it to the roof of the factory and were rescued by profes-sors from the New York University Law School next door, who used ladders to bridge them to safety.

Other workers weren't as fortunate. Under too much pressure, the fire escapes began to buckle. Workers jumped from the burning building. Once the fire department arrived, it only took eighteen minutes to extinguish the flames, but eighteen minutes was too long for the 146 employees who lost their lives to the fire.

In the aftermath, employees and city managers said the Triangle Shirt-waist Factory fire was "an accident waiting to happen." I don't know about you, but when I list the worst ways to die, near the top of the list is burning to death.

There is a fierce anger and reaction to fire. Angry mobs ignite build-ings and businesses when anger erupts with no reasonable outlets to ven-tilate their frustrations. When governments want to repress ideas, they burn books and sometimes people. Burning is irreversible, lifeless. After something's burned, there's no possibility of being rebuilt or reanimated.

When it's burned, it's burned.

Ashes.

Nothing.

I don't want anything I love reduced to embers. Do you?

Jello Biafra wants to do to the church what happened at the Triangle Shirtwaist Factory.

Yet, I suppose there are worse outcomes. At least Jello cares.

"I'll Never Go to Church"

Nicole couldn't muster the energy to care enough about a church to want to burn it.

I'd prefer it if she wanted to start a fire. She didn't.

It was the lack of anger that hung in the air like the tense silence at the end of the last note of a beautifully stunning song. Without a hint of hurt, malice, or irritation, Nicole, a seventeen-year-old high school senior said, "When I turn eighteen and leave home, I'll never step inside another church."

"Why?" I asked, already knowing.

"Because I'm a Democrat and the church doesn't like Democrats. There's no place for us here."

If Nicole were mad I could lasso the typical excuses pastors give when church folks get angry. "It's on them. They have issues. Something deeper must be going on. They don't love God."

Nicole wasn't mad.

Spirit and mind sprinted to locate her absent emotions, but I couldn't. Perhaps she's pissed-off about our congregation's stance on women's roles. That'd be easy. I could tell her how I thought the church was wrong, too. About how complicated the issue is given our history and inherited theology. I could explain how the church—dragged across the finish line like it was with desegregation and slavery—was changing. Dare I say, evolving? I'd heard this objection before. I'd even voiced it a few times myself. I could fix this for her. Our city boasted several churches that practiced differently than we did. Nicole could go to one of those. Don't leave *the* church, just leave *this* church.

Nicole didn't care about gender roles. Small potatoes.

If gender issues weren't irritating her, I wondered, maybe it was homosexuality. I knew Nicole had gay friends. All of our teenagers at church had gay friends. It was a reality as plain as day but stridently ignored by older church leaders whose children were oftentimes older than I was.

Nicole was offended, but not entirely shocked, when one of our church leaders made a thoughtless and cruel joke about homosexuals from the pulpit one Sunday morning. You know the one? Adam and Steve. It's a joke so palpably offensive that only the most dim-witted fail to realize it's not even particularly funny. I was embarrassed that Sunday, too, as a guest of another member, a young man I suspected was gay, stood up and walked out.

I spent two weeks cleaning up that mess. I did for our wounded guest the same thing I wished I could do for Nicole. I pointed him to a church where he could be who he was and continue to walk with God in a community where he'd be less likely to be injured. I could only pledge to him that my words would be seasoned with grace and welcome. However, I couldn't speak for others.

He left the church. Nicole was leaving.

Being only seventeen, I thought perhaps Nicole simply wanted to dabble on the wild side. Roam free. Sow oats. Rock and roll all night. Kids do that. What teenager doesn't get hungry for independence as the aroma of autonomy wafts nearby?

Nope. I'd missed the mark again. Nicole had her early adult life planned. She was disciplined and steadily worked toward her goals in the time I'd known her. Obviously, she'd cut a little loose when Mom and Dad weren't just down the hall. Most of us do. But a small series of rebellions had little to do with Nicole *never* stepping into a church again.

Nicole's affect was flat, matter-of-fact. Her voice carried the same intensity and intonation of a young musician learning his scales. Eight notes up. Eight notes down. Nothing special. Sure, you could jazz it up. Throw in an arpeggio once in a while, but its ultimately the sounds you create to master more moving music later. Nicole's voice was as exciting as a yawn. That's how she said it, "I'll never step inside another church."

Wes

My chauffeur and compadre throughout high school, Wes, became a professional musician while avoiding finding a real job. Wes plays jazz trombone, and if we still lived in a world where people bought CDs, you might flip open a CD jacket and see Wes's name listed as a composer or arranger. Wes was gifted almost from birth. He was first chair in all our high school bands. I was second chair—a distant second chair.

On his way to playing, teaching, and composing music, Wes toured with a contemporary Christian band who needed a horn section. Not every "Christian" band is actually Christian and that's particularly true of the hired guns playing in the horn section. Having been around musicians my entire life, I know the best way to get cancer from second-hand smoke is spending too many hours with the horn section.

The band that hired Wes was a mixed bunch. A few of the guys were straight from the conservative, evangelical casting office. They looked and sounded like the caricature of Christians so popular on TV. These guys felt called to be half-pastor, half-politico and made a point of letting everyone know where they stood and how unrighteous everyone who wasn't them was. Other band members were the artist types, finding life and meaning in constant deconstruction and disruption wherever they saw it. Whether it was inside or outside the church, they lived in a state of constant critique. And then, there were guys like Wes.

Wes was raised a member of a local Methodist church. Like most kids raised in the American South, his family was active at their congregation. Wes's mom and dad hauled Wes and his sister, Eve, to the church where they taught Bible class, served on committees, and drank terrible church coffee. Twenty-five years after Wes and I first met, his parents are still a vibrant part of the same church. Wes never seemed eager about church nor being Methodist.

Methodism seemed nice to me, though. Unlike my church, the Methodists allowed me to play my trombone during worship. I worshipped with Wes's church nearly every Easter and Christmas during high school. They paid me to play my trombone. Forty bucks was nice for a sixteen-year-old kid with no other discernible skills. Having been raised in a non-liturgical congregation, I wasn't used to robes and hand bells and separate pulpits for Scripture reading and preaching. Wes never seemed enamored with it all. It was nonsense to him. I loved it.

After high school, Wes's church life was occasional, and that's probably generous. Like Nicole, Wes wasn't angry with the church. There were no demons to be exorcised. Wes struggled with the reasoning and rationality of faith. He couldn't navigate the learned science of our world and the interpretations of the Bible that he'd been given. Faith left his intellect unoccupied.

Wes isn't a part of any church or community of faith. When I talk to him, he argues that though he and his family aren't a part of a church or synagogue, that he didn't abandon the faith. He just left the church. I don't know all the reasons Wes left the church, but I know touring with a Christian band and playing music in churches filled with that he calls "narrow-minded, mean sheeple," didn't help. God, the teachings of Jesus, and ethics of Jesus are still warehoused within him, but it was this conversation on tour with this band that finally pulled the lever.

One single conversation was all Wes needed. One conversation steeping with thoughtless, hurtful words about homosexuals served up by the band's lead singer birthed Wes's decision. "Those faggots are ruining this country. They should be stoned." Wes just wasn't going to be a part of this callous, deprecating faction.

Duck and Cover

Nicole and Wes entered my life twenty-five years and a continent apart from one another. They shared the same thoughts and dismissal of the Christian church. Church people are discourteous and abrasive. For them, returning the church's animosity or advocating for change wasn't worth the energy. Lacking any vitriol, they each made a choice that whatever the church was, they weren't going to be a part of it.

I wished to heaven that either of them thought the church was irrelevant or misguided about some social or political issue; maybe I could have walked them back from the precipice. If only there were some personal slight—real or perceived—I could have offered an apology for. There wasn't.

Nicole and Wes were running from the same collapsing structure—a church that had ceased being about embrace and was increasingly preoccupied with exclusion and verbal flagellation.

They were leaving a community that disdained differences. Nicole was a Democrat, an unforgivable sin to many in her church. The church that raised her, somewhere along the way, told her they didn't want people like her. She felt their disdain. Every frustrated guest who packed up and walked out confirmed what she believed. Church is for one kind of person—white, straight, middle-class, Republican—and she wasn't that.

When Wes was on tour, words like "gay" and "fag" were common insults in nearly all of the culture. We were less sensitive and less human then. Not understanding what I was doing, I plopped down hurtful words all the time as a high school and college student. No one in my church youth group nor at my Christian college seemed to mind, or even notice that language. Even at that, Wes knew the kind of language deployed by the Christians in the band he was working for was intended to pack more punch than the conventional jabs we had all become desensitized to. The mean-spiritedness was designed to reduce and degrade. They were intended to wound.

Wes was done.

For Nicole and Wes, along with scores of others, the church is a group of people either unwilling or unable to perform the very acts of love the Jesus they were taught about in Sunday school did so readily—heal, embrace, and bless women and men made in the image of God.

Both have seen the church duck and cover from her intended calling. They've seen Christians, myself included, rush to build walls and go to battle. Jello Biafra wants to burn a church, but for Nicole and Wes, the church is not worth the trouble of making and throwing Molotov cocktails.

Slow Burn

Somewhere between Jello Biafra and Nicole and Wes lay an increasing number of people I know and love. Burning the church (maybe even with a few Christians inside) has a growing appeal to some. Others find Christianity so pitiful, anti-everything, and mean-spirited that the best cure is to ignore it altogether. Ignore it and it will go away.

When it comes to church, we're all going to have to think differently. The church doesn't need to be burned or ignored. It needs to be restored. And restored as a church, not like so many of our contemporary attempts to simply "do life together," whatever that means. We need a sweeping reimagining of what the church is in order to shed the political, cultural, and power-thirsty barnacles that have latched onto us.

What we have now, what many of our friends and family members who are striking their matches at the base of church buildings know as the church, is not church. We have lost our original glory and exchanged it for a bloc of predetermined cultural conditions.

When the Bible mentions "church," it's not talking about what we associate with church—buildings, pastors, programs, doctrinal statements and such. Rather, it's talking about Christians serving and loving the world together.

Both the vehemence and apathy toward the church have been created by a long, slow burn ignited—oddly enough—by Christians. For an extended period of time, Christians and vocal, public Christian leaders, in an ill-advised scheme to maintain cultural dominance and control, have twisted the church into an ever-restrictive knot. The first practitioners of Christianity would find what we consider church unrecognizable.

This tangle Christians created erupted from one central, misguided longing—the desire to possess an empire. An empire where certain races,

genders, classes, lifestyles, and practices are privileged. An empire designed to maintain power and nurture a system of allies and enemies.
An empire built by a populace armed with anger, vitriol, criticisms, and
sometimes, weapons.

The temptation to power is as old as humanity itself. As Henri Nouwen reminds us, "Every time we see a major crisis in the history of the
Church, such as the great schism of the tenth century, the Reformation
of the sixteenth century, or the immense secularization of the twentieth
century, we always see that a major cause of rupture is the power exercised
by those who claim to be followers of the poor and powerless Jesus." Rather
than the version of power that dominates, God's church is called to dismiss
power for the sake of the community and the Other. There's never been
another community of people dedicated to enfranchising and empowering
others. History doesn't record a nation or nationality who determined to
appraise their standard of living by how they treated the poorest and lowest.
Few are the chronicles of communities that cared deeply for those on the
other side of the aisle or the other side of the fence.

The archives of mortals only know one people—what Paul calls "one
new humanity"—instructed to care for all people, heedless of self-concern,
power, or personal sacrifice. That group is the church.

At this moment in history, the church I love, the church that supported and nurtured me and my faith is in critical condition. Our supposed
caretakers lost their concern for God's priorities and turned their attention
to constructing their own pyramids of power. We let a few vocal leaders
agitate the rest of the church into a frenzy of behaviors antithetical to the
teachings of Jesus.

For a long time, we've unwittingly played along.

We've played along when we were told that to be moral we should join
a majority of the angry who believed in upholding an extremely narrow
view of what Christianity was and who could be Christian. We kept silent
for years as it was suggested to us that faith-commitments were limited to a
set of ballot propositions and an approved list of candidates. As the church,
we have allowed ourselves to be lulled to sleep by the siren song of winning
some kind of "culture war," and in the process we've lost both the culture
and the church.

In 2012, the Pew Research Center reported that one-fifth of Americans, about forty-six million adults, self-reported no affiliation with church.
In those moments, it's easy for Christian leaders to thrust our arms into the

typical grab bag of excuses. "People aren't interested in faith. It's the gay agenda. Working moms. Democrats. The media. Fundamentalists. They took God out of school."

All of this obscures the truth. The church itself is partly at fault if people want to burn or ignore us. We have failed to be the church, and folks don't need highly sensitive failure detectors to know it. But at the same time, the church is a beautiful, glorious body that is capable of partnering with God to nurture our fallen world.

I love the church—past, present, and future—and I want others to love her, too.

It is time for Christians to go back to church. It's time for us to rescue the alluring, compelling, and welcoming community Jesus intended. This is our opportunity to stop constructing edifices of division and federations of control. It's time for hospitality. It's time for reconciliation. It's time for an unarmed empire.

2

The New Story We Already Knew[1]

We did not hesitate to call our movement an army. But it
was a special army, with no supplies but its sincerity, no
uniform but its determination, no arsenal except its faith,
no currency but its conscience.

—Martin Luther King Jr., *Why We Can't Wait*

"PEOPLE AREN'T INTERESTED IN the church." Over the last few years
those words were spoken, emailed, and even shouted at me as I shared
the desire to articulate something that might help Christians become the
unarmed empire envisioned in the New Testament. "What people want are
simple, straightforward tips they can immediately use; something they can
stick in their back pocket and take home." Disinterest in church life was
the overwhelming sentiment boomeranged back to me when I talked to
people about the need to talk to others about church. Editors could not sell
it. Publishing houses would not print it. Conferences wanted messages that
felt more "sticky."

Institutions aren't in vogue. We live in a time when even the most
long-standing associations are under inquisition.

While consuming movies, books, and music designed primarily for
Christians, it's impossible to miss a certain self-centeredness at the heart of
the Christian enterprise. The same is true even of the events in our week that
are "churchy," like our local, online, and televised worship experiences. We
are chiefly interested in the personal—and often privatized—expressions

1. This chapter first appeared as a sermon co-written between myself and my friend,
Jonathan Storment.

of faith. The church, then, is only useful insofar as it serves our individual purposes. Our language and actions give us away.

What do Christians signal and mean by our actions when we abandon one local community to shop for another once we conclude, "We weren't being fed," or the pastor offends our fragile sensibilities with an offhand comment or challenging message? Personal spiritual growth is certainly a critical aspect of Christian life, but not the only one. Personal spiritual growth, while necessary, cannot reach its objective when it becomes disconnected from the local church. We just don't think the two are connected. Most parents would bristle at the thought of their child ditching the family altogether because they didn't like the vegetables that were served for dinner. Increasingly, Christians feel neither allegiance nor obligation to their churches. That's not surprising when you realize the American church can often morph itself into just another organization in which its members participate. When we grow weary of the "product," we look for something new and improved. It's not that we owe our congregations a blood oath or that we should never leave a local church. I simply continue to be amazed by how easily we do it. Somewhere along the line we became the kinds of people for whom the church means very little.

We're a promiscuous people.

At the same time we bemoan the undeniable fact that Christians wield decreasing influence and power in our culture. Fewer and fewer people value the church, the Christian message, or the highly privileged status enjoyed by Christians in the American story. But the erosion of the church's cultural significance wasn't launched from Hollywood, the academy, or any of the thousands of convenient scapegoats Christians love to blame. The ship of waning prestige set sail from the church itself.

Our culture has rejected church because Christians rejected it first! What if all this talk about "personal salvation" obscures the fact that the church isn't fundamentally about us? What if the purpose of the church is to transform us into the kinds of people who introduce healing and reconciliation in life's most desperate situations? And not just in a sharing and caring sense, but in an indispensable sense. What if it's impossible to follow Jesus alone? What if we need each other the way a hand needs fingers and an opposable thumb? What if we need the tension and cooperation to function?

The church has landed at this moment in history because in the rush of contemporary life and under the disenchantment of the myriad ways our world is broken, we fail to see how meaningful and transforming the church should be for the world.

For starters, we need to recapture what "church" means. If notions of "church" conjure images of uptight people in uptight clothes singing uptight hymns and listening to long-winded, irrelevant sermons given by an uptight preacher, we've missed the heart of it. Church is a community of people animated by the wild, unpredictable spirit of God unleashed to bless the world through love, healing, joy, repentance, and reconciliation. The church is a people, like the Blues Brothers, on a "mission from God," and this mission seeks no less than to tie all the tattered strands of life together under the loving rule of God. This rule of God is called God's kingdom.

Part of God's kingdom is expressed through worship and the sacraments—the part many think of when we imagine "church" to be those uptight people in their uptight pews—but other expressions of church beautifully occur in other places: feeding the hungry, healing the sick, befriending the alien and stranger, faithful presence with the dying, and releasing hope to the broken. This is church too! All these expressions serve an underlying purpose: *reconciliation*. And only the church can accomplish reconciliation. And I do mean *only*. Reconciliation is our purpose, not merely a side project or another program vying for volunteers, attention, and a budget line.

In August 2015 I joined nineteen other ministers and leaders from my denomination for what we called a "Social Justice Bus Ride." For three days we were on a whirlwind tour of a few of the more meaningful sights from the American civil rights movement. Ten members of the group were Caucasian. Ten were African-American. It was all very *Remember the Titans*. We joined together because we believe the rampant enmity, disunity, and division tearing at our world and largely neglected by Christians can only be remedied by the power of God working through churches deeply committed to the rule of God.

The church's ineffectiveness is not bred simply by the Christian's disinterest in her purpose. The deeper cause is because we have lost our story; the story of reconciliation. To recover the Christian story, we have to see the red line of reconciliation that runs through history's greatest story. And, of course, it all starts in the garden.

The Never-Ending Story

The very first story of murder is the story of Cain and Abel. They get in the first ever worship war. Cain raises up and kills his brother, and like his father before him, Cain hides from God. But what's incredible about Cain and Abel is how they are introduced to us. "Eve went on to give birth to Cain's brother, Abel. Abel grew up to become a shepherd, and Cain grew up to become a farmer" (Gen 4:2 The Voice).

In contrast, when we first meet Adam and Eve, we are introduced to them by their similarities. Eve is literally made from the exact same stuff that makes Adam. Where Adam was made from the ground, the dust, Eve was made from Adam. When the first human is introduced into the story in Genesis 1 he is simply called *'ādām*, which means "humankind." In the retelling of creation that follows in Genesis 2, Adam is again referred to by a generic masculine noun, *ish*, which means "man," or "human being." Eve is then called *ishah*—which means "woman," and carries the same root as *ish*, only with a feminine ending. They are more alike than different.

> He formed a woman from the rib taken out of the man and presented her to him.
> Adam: At last, a suitable companion, a perfect partner.
> Bone from my bones.
> Flesh from my flesh.
> I will call this one "woman" as an eternal reminder
> that she was taken out of man. (Gen 2:22–23 The Voice)

From the starting gun, sin's devious ambition is to tear at the seams of God's world. The first symptom of sin's distortions is drawing lines of differences between people. That's the power of sin. Sin wants humankind to embrace, and be defined by, our differences! And because we are blind to Satan's cause, we tend to fall for the trap. Not only do we identify ourselves by our differences, we often love them and build walls to protect them. Sin always divides the world. It divides the world by race, gender, and economics. We are so used to it, we no longer see it.

But that's not how the Bible begins. The Bible does not begin with the creation of a special race of people. Other than gender—a distinction Genesis uses to articulate how humankind will procreate—we know nothing of the differences between the first couple. Adam and Eve are not black, white, or Mexican, not even Jewish. These details, which many folks have spent millions of dollars and countless hours attempting to discern, are unimportant to the narrator, likely because the narrator assumes they are unimportant to the story.

When Genesis 10 tells us about the roll call of nations, it is the first time we learn about divisions between people. That story is immediately followed by the story of the tower of Babel.

In Exodus, the next book of the Bible, Moses—one of the greatest leaders in the history of Israel—marries a Cushite woman, an Ethiopian. It's Scripture's first interracial marriage, and Moses' siblings, Miriam and Aaron, don't like it. For her racism, God gives Miriam a form of leprosy that turned her skin white!

Miriam, like many of us, lost her story. Having just been freed from systematic, race-based slavery in Egypt, Miriam adopts the same difference-based, racially-charged philosophy that had keep the Hebrews shackled for four hundred years. And now we learn that the problem isn't that Egyptians are racist enslavers, but that power-laden racial divisions are a crisis that runs through human blood. The same people who were just delivered from this evil have it in themselves, too.

It gets worse.

In the book of Judges, the racism of the Jews isn't just for non-Jews; it's also for people who aren't the *right* kind of Jews. In Judges 12 the Israelites become racist against other Israelites! They begin murdering people who aren't in their tribe. Miriam's amnesia about Israel's story has now infected the entire tribe of Gilead. The men of Gilead kill as many Ephraimites as they can find.

To ensure there are no survivors, the men set up a gate complete with gate-keepers to sort out the Ephramites. But since they're all Jews, the easy exteriors of race aren't accessible. That's when the men of Gilead remember that the Ephramites have an accent (no funny accents around here!) and there is a certain word they can't say—"Shibboleth."

> Then the Gileadites took the fords of the Jordan against the Ephraimites. Whenever one of the fugitives of Ephraim said, "Let me go over," the men of Gilead would say to him, "Are you an Ephraimite?" When he said, "No," they said to him, "Then say Shibboleth," and he said, "Sibboleth," for he could not pronounce it right. Then they seized him and killed him at the fords of the Jordan. Forty-two thousand of the Ephraimites fell at that time. (Judg 12:5–6)

Forty-two thousand men were killed. That's a virtual holocaust. Why were they killed? Because somewhere in the mind of the men of Gilead the Ephraimites had become inferior because of a difference. Their difference, somehow, made them less human. Gilead had forgotten that it all began with 'ādām, humankind.

But it gets worse.

The book of Jonah isn't about a whale. The church has reduced it to flannel graph and Vacation Bible School because we are scandalized by the extent of God's willingness to reconcile. The whale's tale is about forgiveness and the frustrating nature of God who forgives and loves all the wrong people.

Jonah is the prophet of Israel, and he's either unapologetically racist or a hyper-nationalist. Either way, when God calls Jonah to go preach to Israel's enemy, the Ninevites, Jonah doesn't want to go. And doesn't! While most preachers worry that their hearers won't listen, Jonah's worried his listeners will. He doesn't want "those people" to be forgiven by God.

What a strange brew. Jonah knows YHWH to be a loving and gracious God, and he wants nothing to do with the extension of that love and grace. It is possible, then, to know that God is love, but recuse yourself from it. It is possible to know who God is and what God is doing, but exclude yourself from joining it. This is the definition of "anti-Christ." Jonah is angry at God because God doesn't treat his enemies like he wants God to. As Anne Lamott says, "You can safely assume you've created God in your own image when it turns out God hates all the same people you do."[2]

With this as the backstory, it's not surprising that when Jesus arrives on the scene, his first task is for his people to regain their story; division and enmity between people becomes his first sermon topic. After impressing the good, loyal temple-goers with his reading skills, Jesus reminds them of their story:

> And he said, "Truly I tell you, no prophet is accepted in the proph-
> et's hometown. But the truth is, there were many widows in Israel
> in the time of Elijah, when the heaven was shut up three years and
> six months, and there was a severe famine over all the land; yet
> Elijah was sent to none of them except to a widow at Zarephath
> in Sidon. There were also many lepers in Israel in the time of the
> prophet Elisha, and none of them was cleansed except Naaman
> the Syrian." When they heard this, all in the synagogue were filled

2. Lamott, *Traveling Mercies*, 22.

with rage. They got up, drove him out of the town, and led him
to the brow of the hill on which their town was built, so that they
might hurl him off the cliff. (Luke 4:24–29)

Jesus is an old school prophet. If people aren't trying to kill you, you're
probably not preaching well. And why were the folks at the temple out for
blood? Jesus reminded them of God's blessings on a widow and a soldier,
neither of whom were Jewish. "Outsiders Blessed" was Jesus's sermon title,
and the congregation revolted. What started with Cain and Abel centuries
earlier was still splintering itself more deeply into the human heart. They'd
come to believe that every difference was a meaningful distinction. The
same Jesus they had just been amazed by was more than they could take.

That's the way it happens. When people begin talking about bringing
insiders and outsiders, this group and that group together, the power of
Satan begins to stir. It's as true now as it was then, and we see it on the news
every morning. People who are interested in fences and walls and division
are not on the side of Jesus, and the Lord wanted us to know that from his
very first sermon.

But Jesus doesn't stop there.

Just a few chapters later, Jesus tells one of the more popular parables
in Scripture, the Good Samaritan (Luke 10:25–37). Jesus was asked, "Since
we all know we are supposed to love our neighbor, Who is our neighbor?"
In response, Jesus tells the story of a man who is beaten and robbed and
stripped naked.

The beaten man is unconscious. He can't talk. You can't hear his accent or which language he speaks. He's stripped naked, so you can't see
any identifying clothes or religious identity markers on his clothes. The
bloody unconscious man is unknown. No one knows if he's a Jew or a
Roman. He's just a man. And Jesus tells the story in a way that lets us put
ourselves in his shoes.

If you were about to die, who would you be okay with saving you? The
Samaritan bandages him and pays for his medical care and lodging. In a
world where Jews hated Samaritans—Jews saw Samaritans as half-breeds,
as subhuman—Jesus makes a Samaritan the hero of the story. And then
Jesus asks,

> "Which of these three, do you think, was a neighbor to the man
> who fell into the hands of the robbers?" He said, "The one who
> showed him mercy." Jesus said to him, "Go and do likewise." (Luke
> 10:36–37)

The scholar can't even say the word *Samaritan*. That's how powerful hatred born of divisions runs.

But it gets worse.

Later in John 8, religious leaders are accusing Jesus. They accuse Jesus of being demon-possessed *and* a Samaritan.

> The Jews answered him, "Are we not right in saying that you are a Samaritan and have a demon?" Jesus answered, "I do not have a demon; but I honor my Father, and you dishonor me." (John 8:48–49)

Accusing Jesus of being a Samaritan is an applause line. The enemy has been identified. It's the foreigner, the outsider, the one you can label. And once you can label someone, you can overlay any kind of sinister motivations and stereotypes on them. But Jesus doesn't cooperate with their demagoguery. He doesn't go along with their assumption that to be a Samaritan was shameful or second-class. Jesus simply says, "I do not have a demon." The Lord refuses to entertain their bias.

Remember when Jesus turned over the tables in the Temple? Once again, God tries to call us back to our deeper story. Jesus entered the court of the Gentiles and saw how Jewish religious leaders had turned the court into a marketplace. Gentiles, traveling from all over the region, arrived in Jerusalem without money to purchase animals to make their offering at Passover. They were coming to worship the God of Israel. But some Jews were crowding them out, colluding to drive up prices. Yet another mechanism to privilege insiders and punish outsiders. So, even though this becomes the final straw for the Pharisees, leading to Jesus's arrest and execution, Jesus turns over the tables, saying, "It is written, 'My house will be a house of prayer for all people,' but you have turned this house of prayer into a den of robbers" (Matt 21:13).

God's house was always supposed to be a house of prayer for all nations. That's the story. God's dream has always been for all people.

The Story That's Always Been

The witness of Scripture testifies that God-followers easily forget. Abraham was supposed to be the father of all nations, but he wasn't. The God of Israel was supposed to be known as a God for all people, but he wasn't. And things got worse and worse and worse.

Until . . .

Until . . . Jesus is killed!

These days we talk frequently about divisions, sexism, racism, ethnocentrism, and intersectionality, but we rarely ask why they are important. Until Jesus is killed, as this brief sketch of Scripture demonstrates, no one thought racism, segregation, and classism were wrong. No one thought sexism or ethnocentrism were wrong. No one.

But God did! And it's central to the meaning of the cross. Though it's one of the indications the contemporary church has lost our story, the Apostle Paul never shared our ambiguity about the cross' purpose in recapturing humankind's oneness.

> He is the embodiment of our peace, sent once and for all to take down the great barrier of hatred and hostility that has divided us so that we can be one. He offered His body on the sacrificial altar to bring an end to the law's ordinances and dictations that separated Jews from the outside nations. His desire was to create in His body one new humanity from the two opposing groups, thus creating peace. Effectively the cross becomes God's means to kill off the hostility once and for all so that He is able to reconcile them both to God in this one new body. (Eph 2:14–16)

It Takes One to Know One

Paul recognizes this reconciling work of the cross because, perhaps, he is Scripture's most vivid example of finding God's story after losing it.

Paul, then called Saul, arises in the dusty haze of the religious fallout from Jesus's crucifixion determined to kill every Christian he could find. He was essentially the Jewish ISIS of his day, killing religious Others if they failed his narrow and rigid religious test. He was a racist hyper-nationalist whose only problem with walls was that the lukewarm didn't build them high enough. But Saul has an encounter with Jesus on the road to Damascus, and learns two things: (1) that Jesus really is alive and has defeated death, and (2) that he (Saul) has killed people who were the people of God.

Imagine if this is you. In some ways it may be. How many Christians are participating in words and deeds they believe are to the glory of God, but aren't? How many times have we excluded, condemned, advocated for policy against, or even taken violent action against other people because, like Paul and the millions before him, we lost our story. When we lose the story, we lose God.

On the road to Damascus, Paul discovers he was wrong. He had blood on his hands. He stood exposed as a man who actually hated God because he maligned and killed people made in the image of God. And in response to his sin, Paul does what many refuse to do. He doesn't deny the story that has always been. He doesn't double-down on xenophobia and the low-hanging fruit of exclusion based on the fear of Others. Instead, Paul becomes the chief spokesman for God's very old plan.

Paul is called "the Apostle to the Gentiles" precisely because he becomes animated by the story God's people forgot. Since Paul was Cain that had just killed his brother, he goes all over the world planting churches of the new people of Abraham, the father of all nations. Paul also becomes the reverse Jonah. He becomes the new Shibboleth gatekeeper, but he makes sure the gate stays open for all. Paul goes to the widows of Isaiah, to the foreigner and families of the wife of Moses, to launch new communities dedicated to the rule of God. Paul builds new temples to be houses of prayer for all nations. He goes all over the world telling people about the family of Abraham and calling people with whom he has no blood relationship "brother" and "sister." He tells everyone about the King of the Universe named Jesus. He's the first person in human history proclaiming that Jews and Gentiles, slave and free, male and female, were equal and free. If you're a Gentile and believe the God of Israel is the Creature of the Universe, it's because Paul took the Gospel out of the thirty-mile radius of Judea and preached that *you* could come in. Paul calls this new community of loved and accepted persons *the church*.

A Church of a Different Kind

On the "Social Justice Bus Ride" I mentioned earlier, our group spent a morning at 16th Avenue Baptist Church in Birmingham, Alabama. Students of American history will remember a bomb that exploded at 16th Avenue on September 15, 1963. If you've seen the movie *Selma*, the first scene recounts that bombing. The bomb was made of fifteen sticks of dynamite and placed underneath the church steps. It was designed and planted by four white supremacists—Thomas Edwin Blanton Jr., Herman Frank Cash, Robert Edward Chambliss, and Bobby Frank Cherry—and killed four girls—Addie

Mae Collins, Carole Robertson, Cynthia Wesley, and Denise McNair. The girls were preparing for worship when the blast went off.

Walking around 16th Avenue, a question you might ask yourself is, "Why would someone bomb a church?" Or, more recently, "Why would Dylan Roof walk into Emmanuel AME Church on June 17, 2005, to shoot and kill nine people?"

But as I thought about it, I realized that the bombers, Dylan Roof, and others throughout history got their target right. When it comes to freedom, equality, and dignity for all people, that idea comes from the gospel. It comes from the story that was lost and the story Jesus helps us regain.

One of the more stunning sites you'll see if you visit 16th Avenue Baptist is a stained-glass window of Jesus. The window is thirty to forty yards from where the blast went off on September 15. Remarkably, there was no damage to it, except for the blown out face of Jesus. There was just a hole—no mouth, no nose, no lips, and no eyes—like someone had cut it out like a kind of cardboard cut-out you might see at a state fair. There was no face of Jesus, which seems right. Jesus turns his face away from every effort to pull the world apart.

The people who want to bomb a church, like Miriam, Jonah, the Ephraimites, and religious leaders, want to bomb it because they dislike who God allows in it. They lost the story. But if a church isn't a house of prayer for all nations, it's not a church at all.

All the people who "just aren't interested in church" have lost the plot. They only think they want something more action-oriented and relevant than what they think church is. But nothing is more relevant to our country and our world than the church living God's story. In fact, the greatest moves for justice and reconciliation in history began in churches.

At the beginning of the civil rights movement, and during the Montgomery bus boycott, thousands of people met for worship every evening. Though they walked to work and school, they still managed to marshal the energy to walk to worship. The Montgomery bus boycott lasted 381 days. For 381 days, protests for justice were launched from the pew. The church was at the center. Even before the march on Washington, leaders and marchers met for worship before setting their faces toward the Capitol. Again, the church was at the center.

The evening Martin Luther King Jr. was assassinated he was walking out of his hotel room in Memphis, headed to dinner then to worship. His last words were to a musician named Ben Branch. King said, "Ben, make sure you play 'Take My Hand, Precious Lord' in the meeting tonight. Play it real pretty."

The story of God—a story of a welcoming, hospitable people extending grace to all who come—didn't start in Washington or Montgomery. God's dream of a church that serves the world as an unarmed empire, started in a manger with a Savior sent to help us reclaim our story. It ran through the pen of a church-planter named Paul.

It's the church!

3

Victims of the Discourse, Part 1

I agree with you likewise in your wishes to keep religion
and government independant [sic] of each Other. Were it
possible for St. Paul to rise from his grave at the present
juncture, he would say to the Clergy who are now so active
in settling the political Affairs of the World: "Cease from
your political labors—your kingdom is not of *this* World.
Read my Epistles. In no part of them will you perceive me
aiming to depose a pagan Emperor, or to place a Christian
upon a throne."

—Benjamin Rush to Thomas Jefferson, October 6, 1800

S TARING AT MY BANK account in the fall of 2008, I knew I needed to
find a job. After nearly ten years living and working in Houston, the
congregation I worked for decided to eliminate my position.

They told me in September, right after I had returned from an out-
of-town trip, but planned to keep me on staff until May. It was a grace not
many pastors get. I had eight months to land on my feet. I had friends
who had been "eliminated" before; a few barely got eight hours. They were
unceremoniously walked out or given until the end of the week to clear
their desks. Regardless, it was not the kind of news I wanted to share with
my wife, Rochelle.

We weren't in the best financial spot when the news came down. Rochelle had stopped working full-time five years earlier after the birth of our
first daughter, Malia. A year and a half before my "elimination," she'd given
birth to our second daughter, Katharine. The money we'd saved during

the early days of our marriage was steadily seeping through the cracks of school loans, a mortgage, two car payments, and four mouths to feed. Finances were tight and getting tighter. We weren't the only ones. At the time the housing market and economy were in the worst shape they had been in since the Great Depression. We'd been living on one income, and that income was coming to an end.

Long before September 2008, both our church and family knew a parting of the ways was headed our direction. On any given day, one of us could have looked at the other and said goodbye. We'd grown apart and that was fine. It happens. There are pushes and pulls in life. I'd felt pulled in a new direction for a while, but this was the push I needed. We were like a couple that had been together for a long time, but knew they would never get married; both secretly hoping the other would muster the courage to look in the other's eyes and say what we both knew was true: "It's not you, it's me."

For a while, I had been looking to break free and my church knew it. For four years I had been looking for where God was calling me next. After being turned down by two congregations and turning others down, I needed to fish or cut bait. It was past time to leave. In ministry, going separate ways is sometimes the best means to loving one another. Paul and Barnabas were effective ministers, just not together.

After college, Rochelle and I took the road most traveled for children of the church. Two years into marriage I had gone to work for a mid-sized congregation in Houston and Rochelle was practicing her craft as a counselor for students at a school for children with diagnosed learning differences. Life was just how I envisioned when I was younger. I was a youth minister at a progressive (for my denomination) church, we'd bought a house in the suburbs, and Rochelle was working with adolescents as a counselor. But that existence became torpor for my soul. Life had become paint-by-numbers and uninspiring. I was restless and wanting an adventure. "Waiting for my real life to begin," as Colin Hay sang.

My ennui was making Rochelle crazy. We were closing in on our mid-thirties and, like many of our friends, we woke up with two dependable Hondas (which we still drive), a house, the mortgage that goes with it, and a question: "Is this as good as it gets?"

We felt tinges of jealousy every Christmas when we poured over Christmas and holiday cards. Friends and relatives made leaps we never considered or were too afraid to entertain. Missionaries in Peru, China, and

Thailand; they were doing *real* stuff. We had friends living courageously and changing their world while I fiddled around perfecting PowerPoint slideshows for Wednesday night Bible class. Don't get me wrong—Wednesday night Bible class is valuable. I wouldn't trade my youth ministry years, nor those kids and families, for anything. Plus, keeping tired, distracted kids engaged with the Word of God is no effortless endeavor. The kids I worked with were priceless, but after thirteen years as a youth pastor, I was ready for something new, something that didn't involve so many fart jokes.

One month before the push came, we stumbled across an opportunity to preach and lead a congregation in California, just outside San Francisco. We jumped through all the usual hoops—résumé, multiple phone interviews, a weekend visit and preaching, and finally the offer, acceptance, and negotiation.

Everything associated with this move just fell into my lap. It all looked orchestrated by God. Christians love the idea of God closing one door and opening another. This is what had to be happening, right? Plus, who wouldn't want to live in one of the more beautiful places on earth, with the best weather in the country, and make a fresh start? But an unforeseen problem arose between the moment we signed the dotted line and the minute we unpacked our boxes in California: A presidential election.

What the TiVO Saw

Generally believing that politicians, regardless of party, are pretty much the same, I had never put much stock in politics. Still don't. I don't wake up in the morning defining myself as a Republican, Democrat, Libertarian, or Green. I was taught in Sunday school that God told Samuel to make sure the Israelites knew that whoever was king, he was going to levy taxes, form armies for war, and be more concerned about his kingdom than their lives. And while there were certainly good and bad, better and worse kings (and queens), God was offended when his people turned to human leaders rather than to him. This was my approach to politics. I trust so little in politics; it's a good election cycle if I remember to vote at all.

The year 2008 was different. Three years earlier, Rochelle—while I was away with teens at camp—heard a young(ish) Senator from Illinois speak at the Democratic National Convention. At that time, Barack Obama seemed like a breath of fresh air, even though we had previously voted for and financially supported George W. Bush. We felt the bipartisan spirit and goodwill Bush demonstrated in Texas had been overwhelmed by stagnant and dark forces in Washington. W. had been our governor, and a pretty decent one, we believed. Since his parents, George and Barbara, had deep roots in Houston, many of our friends were his friends. Plus, my father's schoolmate, Dr. Rod Paige, was Bush's Secretary of Education. In more ways than one, we were linked to W., and Rochelle and I believed 9/11 handed Bush a bad deal with few good alternatives. At the same time, we believed the nation and world needed a change.

During the primary season, I caught wind of an organizing meeting for Barack Obama's campaign in Texas. He was standing toe to toe and going blow for blow with Hillary Clinton, and for once the Texas primary was going to matter. I wasn't sold on Barack Obama, but he seemed like the best of all the available choices.

I went to the organizing meeting.

It was unlike anything I had ever experienced.

We gathered on a Wednesday night in a questionable neighborhood on the southeast edge of Houston. If this was the best that Team Obama could do, they were going to get waxed by Hillary's battle-tested and experienced team. But that hot, cinder block room filled with cracked, rusting metal chairs became one of the more heartwarming scenes of my life. We were packed in. About 400 human sardines smashed into a room made for 250. As the meeting started, the organizer, a 30-ish African-American woman with curly, untouched natural hair, asked a few of us to share when and where we first discovered "the candidate." Most folks were like me. I hadn't heard Barack Obama's speech at the 2004 Democratic National Convention, but Rochelle's enthusiasm convinced me to do what I always do when I have a question; read a book. I read Obama's *Audacity of Hope* (that was my introduction to "the candidate). The same was true for over half the room.

It wasn't Obama or his political agenda that stirred my spirit that night. It was the people. The fabric of the people looked like *Joseph's Amazing Technicolor Dreamcoat.* We were black, white, middle-class, wealthy, and poor. And we'd convened in one of the more pauperized neighborhoods in Houston in the hope of having our voices heard. Some of us were classic political liberals. Others, like me, were conservative about almost everything. We all worried that too many people were being left behind by a church and state, which were both consumed with selfish-ambition and we were eager to welcome a new day.

I wondered: Why doesn't *my* church look like this? Not since I was a boy in Mississippi had I seen people who don't belong together *be* together. The packed room was steeped with people looking for some kind of congress, not the political kind, but the actual thing—a coming together of people—working to accomplish something for the greater good. While there was no uniformity of thought, there was a consensus of ideals. This comes as a shock to folks who eat, drink, and sleep partisanship, and it came as a surprise to me too. I was expecting braless "feministas" and angry young anarchists. I was looking for the people I'd heard about when I listened to Limbaugh, Ingraham, and Hannity.

Those folks weren't there.

These people were like me. When they spoke about what they wanted for their country, they wanted what I wanted. Our desires weren't incomprehensible to one another. We were together in more ways than I had imagined.

News cameras were there that night. This could be a problem, I thought. I didn't want anyone to know I was there. I didn't even know how I felt about it, myself. I was fearful about how my church members would feel. This was supposed to be a secret.

My cover was blown. My TV debut occurred on the eleven o'clock news. I was on the screen for less than half a second, but in the age of TiVO, it might have well have been an hourlong special. "Sean Palmer Supports Obama" might as well have been "The Big Story" that night (with all the subtlety of a bat to the head, the local Houston news always dubbed their first story "The Big Story"). I didn't watch the late night news that night. Some folks from my church did.

All hopes of anonymity crashed the following Saturday as several key leaders from our congregation gathered for an all-day meeting. One of our lay leaders approached me saying, "Hey! I saw you on the news."

I'd been outed.

The cardinal rule of ministry—at least in my denomination—is to keep your politics to yourself. I'd broken it. My worst fear had come to fruition. I should've seen it coming. Just twenty-four hours earlier, my phone rang. Blaring through the headset was my dad's thunderous bass. "You're on the front page of Daily Kos, son!" The left-leaning website had picked up an AP photo from the organizing meeting, and there I was, center stage.

My cat had leapt out of its bag. I was supporting a Democrat and everyone at my congregation knew it. I was dead in the water. First would come general, but polite, questions. Next there would be more pointed inquiries about candidates and policies. Ultimately someone would press hard on the two non-negotiables in the minds of many Evangelical Christians: homosexuality and abortion.

Though I'm certain Christians of all stripes and denominations vote for Democrats, I'm equally sure many of them keep quiet about it (but we'll talk about why that is later).

The dread I anticipated was in vain. As a matter of fact, in a few weeks time, I knew everyone in our church who was a Democrat. It was like a secret club. There were no initiation rituals or hazing, but they all knew one another and, I think, traded knowing winks and nods at potlucks. Soon I was invited to lunches and joined in hushed conversations with the Democratic cabal in my congregation.

My Democratic voting friends loved that I was out. It was a relief to them. Relief that their views on American life and politics weren't inherently out-of-line with God and the Jesus story; relief they weren't the odd ducks and weren't crazy drifters in a Republican religious sea. After I was outed, they came out too!

Because I'd been outed, I wrote about Obama at my then fledgling blog, *The Palmer Perspective*. I had thirty-eight faithful readers in those days, and neither readers nor non-readers seemed to care about one vote in one election in dead Red Texas. We all went on with our lives.

Houston is a diverse city. While ethnically we weren't a diverse church, the careers and lifestyles of most of our congregants placed them in seats of influence working alongside women and men of vastly different views at both work and in the public sector. Our church members lived and worked with all kinds of people and, for the most part, had learned to do it well. At the very least, they had learned to be civil.

Our church in Houston didn't really care about my politics. But we didn't live in Houston too much longer after the 2008 election. In February 2008 our family moved to serve a new church just outside of San Francisco. That church cared! A lot.

Turning the Screw

A week after accepting their offer to serve as senior minister, one of my new elders called to ask me about supporting Obama. We hadn't yet bought the first packing box and I was already in trouble. One of their church members had read through every blog post I had written and called him worried about my "judgment." Another member questioned whether the church was "heading in a strange direction." The elder called me wanting to talk things through and have me answer a few questions. "Card-carrying Republican" wasn't on the job description but it should have been! From the first moment my conservative bona fides were found deficient, my ministerial qualifications were under suspicion.

I didn't want to believe my Christianity was in question, but it was. I had dive-dropped into a nest of vocal, hyper-politicized Christians and had not known it. Nearly every question church members asked me during the first year of my tenure was about politics. Without an appointment, books arrived on my doorstep demanding to be seen. "Did you read the book I sent you?" Books written *by* Republicans *for* Republicans collected themselves on my front stoop. My favorites were the ones accompanied by notes assuring me, "This is written by a *black* conservative."

Thomas Sowell sold a lot of books while I lived in California. Being a stone's throw from The Hoover Institute was like having a conveyor belt delivering every article and book penned by the Hoover Fellow directly into my e-mail inbox or front door steps. I wasn't sufficiently conservative.

Message delivered.

Having lived in Texas, my conservative credentials were never questioned. Appearing on the news the previous spring and supporting a Democrat turned out to be a tidbit. We had friendly, open conversations about Obama vs. McCain as well as all manner of global and local politics. Maybe hardcore conservatives in The Lone Star State reckoned that one more Democratic vote in Texas wasn't going to make any difference, so who cared? At the same time, lifelong Democrats in our Houston faith community embraced me like I had finally seen the light. In Texas, who I voted for was information. In California, it was a declaration of war.

I was dumbstruck by my reception. Given the fact that I was living just outside of Nancy Pelosi's San Francisco, I expected a much different welcome. Mark Twain said, "The coldest winter of my life was a summer in San Francisco." Twain's perception of Northern California's weather permeated my time in San Francisco from my first Sunday to my last. The reception was cold and it stayed cold!

Within the first month, the church's elders (lay leaders in my denomination) had already received messages from church insiders: "Wrong guy." Rochelle and I were greeted by rooms struck silent by our entrance. The whispers had all been about us, and we walked in too quickly for anyone to smoothly change the conversation. Every word I uttered was X-rayed and inspected. There was in-depth search for other signs of my sinfulness. Since I approved all congregational announcements during worship services, clever ploys were developed to work around the system so that dedicated politicos could announce where to go online to find conservative voter guides. At least once a month some politically tinged e-mail forward somehow meandered its way into congregational prayers.

In fairness, most of the congregation didn't care who I'd voted for. Yet there were a few heavy hitters who took early, furtive swings. None so much as the elder's wife, Laura, who didn't speak to me for *three years*.

The Code of Silence

During our interview weekend, before electoral votes were cast in November 2008 (and my judgment questioned), Rochelle and I shared warmly with nearly everyone in the church. We had dinner with a large group in Laura's and her husband Rich's home. The night was standard fare: Q and A, sharing our story, and discussing philosophy of ministry. Nothing out of the ordinary. Laura even pulled Rochelle into the kitchen to share the tale of how she and Rich met and a little of what their lives had been like. There was no way we would have guessed that night, after knowing one another for just a few hours, that it was the last time Laura would speak to either of us. After the Obama revelation bubbled to the surface, she never spoke another word to anyone in our family, not even our daughters. Unless we sought her ought directly, there was no conversation. Even those interactions were terse.

Laura only broke her silent treatment once during a church workday, but only briefly. She'd helped prepare lunch for all the workers and by the time she was ready to sit down to eat, all the chairs were taken except one next to me. Panic struck! Laura's eyes darted around the playground and parking lot where we'd set-up tables and chairs, like a driver hunting a parking spot hopeful that someone would be leaving. What could she do? She couldn't just stand there. It was too awkward. Either she had to sit by me or wonder if everyone else was wondering about her *not* sitting by me.

Laura sat down.

Speaking to no one in particular, she launched, "You know, all these 'so-called Christians' who voted for Obama, they are really going to regret it. Now we're going to see nothing but the abortion and the gay-marriage agenda. That Obama is a Muslim. I know it. He wasn't even born here. And now they give him the Nobel Peace Prize because they know he will cut-n-run from Iraq. He has done nothing."

Message delivered.

Again.

If you've ever been so incensed that all you could do is laugh, you know exactly how I felt. (These are the moments that test my fidelity to nonviolent resistance.) She finished her broadside, and I politely excused myself because I grew up in the South and my parents taught me manners like talking to the person you're talking about and respecting your elders. What's more, there was nothing to say, at least nothing that would penetrate her calcified conviction that she was right about everything and everyone.

I knew my vote for Obama, like all votes, would cut both ways. After four years, some of his policies would shape the world for the better, others for the worse, just like all presidents. I harbored no illusions. The difference between Laura and me is that I realized the same thing about my votes four and eight years earlier for George W. I'm not a perfect man, but I refuse to labor under the notion that my vote made me any more or less righteous or Christian. One of the easier postures for religious people is self-righteousness. We have so many good names for religious superiority and naked sanctimony—conviction, belief, truth. Self-righteousness is an effortless bed on which to lie. Who, armed with the truth, would ever ease territory or cede ground to others they believe are wrong?

This was Laura.

All too often, what people like Laura decide to be "truth" though is merely an unfounded justification to devalue a life or lifestyle we wouldn't choose. It is a desire to (re)make the world in our own image, or our own simple refusal to see the image of God in the Other. "*You know, all these 'so-called' Christians.*"

Priggishness, though, has the crippling side effect of quarantining the infected from the havoc it brings to others. We use our twisted views of righteousness to distance ourselves from people the way Laura distanced herself from me. Righteousness, for folks like Laura, requires a polarity. In order to be righteous—which is, after all, a good thing—she must personally define "unrighteous." Once complete it becomes easy to build walls around everything that doesn't fit our definition of righteousness. That's the only way life makes sense. Black and white. Good and bad. I decide which is which.

People like Laura, for me, are emblematic of everything wrong with the church, and why people like Wes and Nicole reject church. Laura and her ilk, in my opinion, are the reason Christians fail to create beloved communities. She is antithetical to everything I was taught about the meaning and mission of Jesus. In my weaker, less faithful, and angrier moments, I question whether Laura can call herself a Christian and say so with any integrity.

And my distaste for her is also part of the problem. Laura and I are cut from the same cloth. We are both victims of the discourse, and it's killing the church.

4

Victims of the Discourse, Part 2

I was born a poor, black child in Mississippi.

—Navin Johnson, *The Jerk*

M Y DISTASTE FOR LAURA wasn't only her problem. No matter how
much I wanted to blame the tension between us on her, I contributed
my part. In many ways, Laura and I are two peas in the same pod. We had
both become victims of the strange, constricting discourse ripping at the
seams of the church. She was a dyed-in-the-wool Conservative. The kind
that is easy to caricature as a frightened old woman plopped in front of Fox
News every day swallowing wholesale whatever anti-Obama, the-Left-is-
the-Devil, anti-science, pro-war, semi-moral morsel Sean Hannity shovels
on any particular day. I'm not sure that caricature exists in reality and it's
certainly not fair, but when I saw Laura, that's who I saw. Laura didn't have
to talk to me in order for us to interact. We just interacted badly. Laura
disliked me because of what she assumed about my politics. I came to
dislike her because of the way she worshipped her politics. Enmity became
our love language.

Like everyone else, I was born into a world in love with differences.
In fact, I was trained in the church not only that differences were relevant,
but that loving and nurturing differences was an essential part of following
God. Rejection was an attitude I learned in church.

I was raised in the small town of Gautier (pronounced, GO-SHAY),
Mississippi. The closest "big" town was Pascagoula, and if it weren't for the
Navy, no one would be able to pronounce the name of that town either. All
the same, I enjoyed growing up on the coast of Mississippi and part of my

heart will always live there. Two images animate my memory as a young boy in the South: playing baseball and my church. I was raised in a small, southern, and conservative religious movement called Churches of Christ.

The Gautier Church of Christ was hardline and hardcore, an old-time religion church of Christ. It was the kind of church people either rejoice in or recover from. Life with that church was in my bones, and my family participated in everything the church did.

When I was eight, my family took a trip to the big city, Biloxi, to hear some big name traveling preacher. It was a treat for my brother, Richard, and me because our family never went out to eat, but, on that night, my parents took us to a seafood restaurant in Biloxi, The Cock of the Walk. We each ordered the buffet, and Richard and I thought we had hit the food lottery. Nothing in life compared to endless seafood in what we thought was a fancy restaurant. Sadly, through the years I've discovered that "fancy" and "buffet" aren't two words usually used together. All the same, it might as well have been a state dinner to Richard and me. We loved The Cock of the Walk; we even loved saying the name. We forced our dad into promising to take us back. He promised. Thirty years later, I'm still waiting for my return visit.

Leaving dinner, I was loaded down with crawfish, hushpuppies, and shrimp. Who cared what some preacher had to say? My night was already a success. The price I had to pay for shrimp-gut was listening to some strange preacher preach. And preach he did!

I can't tell you how long he spoke, but to an eight-year old boy, it felt like forever. As a matter of fact, I think it felt like forever to everybody else too, even my mom, who typically nudged and pinched the rest of us into alertness through boring sermons, drifted off, nodding her head a few times. She'll never admit it, but it's true.

As long as the sermon was, the "invitation song" was even longer. Taking a page from Billy Graham, this preacher cued up the worship leader and apparently wouldn't let him stop singing until some unannounced quota of people made their way down the aisle. The song we sang that night was "Just as I Am." Again, he was a poor man's Billy Graham.

We sang "Just as I Am" for so long that who I was actually changed a few times.

In between each verse, Mr. Preacher would stop the song leader and tell a story about someone who wanted to get baptized or was headed to get baptized, but had a heart-attack or was in a car wreck and never made it to the baptistery. In the church of my childhood, to be "saved" meant being baptized. No more. No less. The night's preacher wanted us to know that without a doubt. After every story Mr. Preacher would cue up the song leader for another verse, hoping this time, maybe, we would finally be scared enough to hop into the water.

We sang "Just as I Am" so long I think some people were baptized, died, and went home to glory before we were done.

Life in the Pew

I carry precious memories from my life with that church. I remember being witness to my father's baptism. One year at Vacation Bible School I won the "Fishers of Men" trophy for bringing the most visitors to church. My mother still has the trophy in her house. I am a child of the church. Much of my life is rooted in the stories of life as a child among those people.

My early days of church life were quirky. As a kid, I didn't know Sunday school was different than regular school. I took God and church seriously. I studied for Bible classes. Because I was well studied, my Sunday school teachers were forced to move me up to the older kids' classes because I outpaced my peers in Bible knowledge.

When my brother was thinking about getting baptized, our preacher came over to the house one summer day to talk with him about it. Richard and I had strict rules about who could come into the house when our parents weren't home: No one! So our preacher stood outside our front door and talked to my brother on the other side.

We had our share of church intrigue, too. A scandal was launched in our little congregation once when our song leader let his unbaptized son take communion. You would've thought the ceiling was going to fall in from the drastic drop in air pressure caused by the church's collective gasp.

And then there was the time when my own family experienced church tumult when my dad was nominated to be a deacon. Some church members objected because my dad didn't attend Wednesday night Bible class. Instead, he was taking night classes at the local university to finish his Masters degree. His priorities were clearly in the wrong place. Dad had placed his education before church and in that place and that time, nothing came before church. Nothing. And I learned those lessons well and early. Our church had a simple orientation toward the world: us against them!

What I remember most is the turbulence inside me when, at five years old, my parents decided to enroll me in a Baptist kindergarten. I thought my parents had slipped off their mental rockers! A "Baptist" kindergarten? Surely they knew better. Hadn't they been paying attention at church? We were the only ones granted passage through the Pearly Gates. How dare they? Baptists believed in "once saved always saved," and our preachers told us how wrong that was. I got that message loud, clear, and frequently.

Yet, Richard Sr. and Gloria pulled the trigger and placed me with the apostates anyway. Each day I'd arrive early for school. My dad dropped me off on his way to work. Every morning, I'd hop out of his brown-yellow 1974 Ford Pinto (that car was ballin'!), and reluctantly walk through the kindergarten doors, sit down in the corner of the large playroom and retreat into my inner world. The teachers barely beat me through the doors. I was always the first student there. As other kids arrived they would get out toys and play together, but I just sat in my corner, wedged between a large, worn, brown, particleboard bookshelf and an even larger counter. I would sit and sing songs to myself, mostly songs I had learned in church: "Softly and Tenderly," "Oh, Why Not Tonight," even "Just as I Am." I suppose I had a thing for what my church called "invitation songs."

I never really engaged the other kids. I kept to myself and hardly ever played with anyone. Those kids were Baptist. Off-limits!

By the time I was five I had been taught that only the people in my church, and churches like ours, were real Christians. I knew at five that those "evil Baptists," with their instrumental music, choirs, choir robes, and "pastors"—not preachers—weren't the kind of people I was supposed to be around. This was a big deal in our home. Even before my parents enrolled me in school, I overheard them discussing it. Christian parents don't discuss their children being around other *real* Christians. I knew I ought to be concerned and prepared not to let the Baptists co-opt the purity of my faith. This was how I approached kindergarten; ready to contend for the faith and make an argument for the hope I had . . . to those Baptists.

That Christmas as my kindergarten was preparing for their annual Christmas pageant, I was vehemently opposed to participating—I said those exact words to my parents too: "I'm vehemently opposed." I had an advanced vocabulary for five. I didn't want to participate in this unbiblical, man-made tradition. Christmas was something "the denominations" did. I wasn't part of "the denominations"—as my church called all the other churches who weren't us. I was part of the "true church."

Unconvinced, my parents forced me into life among the Baptists and their clearly hedonistic Christmas pageant. My parents were obviously not as devoted as I was. If they were they would never have banished their younger son to the land of the Baptists in the first place.

Even at that young age, I could give you book, chapter, and verse for everything my church did, and I knew I was *supposed* to be able to give you book, chapter, and verse. I knew who the real Christians were and the reason I could give you book, chapter, and verse is because when I was a kid, the central question of faith was who is "in" and who is "out." Faith was a debate; faithfulness was about being both right and self-righteous about being right. It was my church versus other churches and which one was the right one, the true one.

Growing up in that way forces you to adopt divisions and self-righteousness as signs of godliness. Laura drew her dividing line along partisan politics. I had been taught as a child to draw mine around religion.

Laura and I represent the natural tendency of people—as we saw running through the entire narrative of the Bible until Jesus—to live in acrimony rather than harmony. This is what Paul has to battle his entire ministry, because it's the central task of being the church. Nowhere is this issue more apparent than in Paul's letter to the church in Rome. Romans—while packed with enough theology to keep readers engrossed for centuries—is ultimately about relationships.

If that sounds like news, don't be shocked. Romans has been misread and reduced to atonement debates for a long time now, but Paul's work has real-world, right-now, flesh-and-blood intent behind it.

Toward the end of his ministry, the Apostle Paul is on the move. Up until now, Antioch has been his home base, but now Paul is looking to expand his territory. Yet there's more than simple missionary zeal behind Paul's move. The church in Antioch has become partisan and divided along racial and religious lines. Paul chronicles the rift in Galatians 2:

> But when Cephas came to Antioch, there was a problem. I got in his face and exposed him in front of everyone. He was clearly wrong. Here's what was going on: before certain people from James arrived, Cephas used to share meals with the Gentile outsiders. And then, after they showed up, Cephas suddenly became aloof and distanced himself from the outsiders because he was afraid of those believers who thought circumcision was necessary.
>
> The rest of the Jewish believers followed his lead, including Barnabas! Their hypocritical behavior was so obvious—their

actions were not at all consistent with everything the good news of our Lord represents. So I approached Cephas and told him in plain sight of everyone: "If you, a Jew, have lived like the Gentile outsiders and not like the Jews, then how can you turn around and urge the outsiders to start living like Jews?" (Gal 2:10–14 The Voice)

Paul needs to get out of town because the Christians in Antioch lacked the get-along gene, and Paul worries his brothers and sisters in Rome may face a similar kind of unraveling. We will return to the Antioch incident later, but there is more going on in Rome than one Apostle's desire to set straight a theology about guilt and grace, though it certainly does that. It's about stemming the human tendency to "distance themselves from outsiders."

We often miss the details of Romans because none of us ever visited Emperor Claudius' Imperial Library & Museum (a place I made up) or sifted through his records and personal diaries (which I don't know if he kept). If we had, we'd learn that Claudius expelled Jews from Rome in 49 AD—though it's unclear if they all left. While many remaining Gentiles were God-followers, unlike the church in Galatia, few were willing to swallow whole cloth the Jewish law. The absence of Jews in and around Rome provided Gentile Christians the space and time to define a Jesus-centered religion without the very Jewish baggage the Roman government found suspicious. But now, Claudius has died (54 AD). Nero is the new Emperor, and Nero doesn't care about much besides Nero—at least for now. When Claudius dies, his decree expelling the Jews dies with him. If you are a Jew from Rome, the exile is over, and all that's left is to pack up your carry-on and head home. If you're a Gentile from Rome, the returning Jews, some still hanging on to many of their long-held Torah practices, were less than a welcomed sight. Division is to be expected.

As Jews stream back into Rome, these scattered churches filled with Gentiles now have to accommodate returning Jews and figure out how to live with one another; how to handle their diversity; how to handle their division.

The Gentiles don't want to listen to Jews clamor on about being the "chosen people" and special and set apart. And the Jews aren't sure about how much they want to deal with these Gentiles and all their nasty, pork-eating Gentile habits.

Paul writes Romans to demonstrate how to get along with people who aren't like us. It's the kind of thing we should learn in kindergarten, but the earliest Christians couldn't conceive of it, and many of us choose not to either. Both then and now our knee-jerk reaction to difference is division.

A difference in accent, skin color, politics, nationality, religion, or just about anything else is enough difference to accept division. Shocking as it sounds, living peacefully with others is what Romans is about. I know there have been enough books, commentaries, and sermons throughout the centuries that reduced Romans to a puzzle of mixed-up and random doctrinal statements and independent clauses, but if that's what Paul was after, he went about it the worst way possible. A checklist would have served us much better. This is about a new kind of community.

For centuries the Jews had been God's people. They were told that God was particular. They knew where the line was drawn. God was with them and against everyone who wasn't them. What's more, God would bring about the Kingdom through the Jews and for the Jews.

Which is only good news if you are a Jew.

The Jews have spent a lot of time waiting for God to come through and deliver the Messiah who will return them to their rightful and privileged place at the head of the class. From Abraham through the Exodus, to the conquering of the Promised Land, to the exile and return, through the Maccabean revolt, and into Roman rule, they have been waiting on a Savior who will be the "King of the Jews" and set the world right. If Jesus is the "King of the Jews," who cares about Gentiles? They've never belonged and they won't ever belong. But now some people coming out of Jerusalem— calling themselves "apostles"—are teaching that Gentiles, all these people Jews have warred against for centuries, all these filthy dogs that haven't kept the law, are now justified before God. Can you imagine how unsettling that might feel? If you can't, a quick viewing of news footage from the integration of southern schools following the *Brown v. Board of Education* ruling in the southern United States will give you an idea. Southern white protestors screaming while holding signs reading, "we want to keep our schools white," and "we won't go to school with negroes," will give you a sense of the turmoil felt when insiders realize that their prejudice is in fact injustice. Pain is what Paul's Jewish readers felt, like so many folks both before and after them—and like Laura and me—they knew where the line was and felt those lines were ordained by God.

And they were wrong!

Paul launches Romans with a scandalous claim:

If, my brothers and sisters, you did not already know, my plans were set to meet you in Rome, but time and circumstances have forced every trip to be canceled until now. I have deeply desired to see some good fruit among you just as I have seen with so many non-Jewish believers. For I am not the least bit embarrassed (ashamed) about the gospel. I won't shy away from it, because it is God's power to save every person who believes: first the Jew, and then the non-Jew. (Rom 1:13–16 The Voice)

Romans casts the church as a large community, a vision that is echoed later in Romans 8:28–29: "We know that all things work together for good for those who love God, who are called according to his purpose. For those whom he foreknew he also predestined to be conformed to the image of his Son, in order that he might be the firstborn within a large family" (NRSV). The New Testament vision of the church is based on belief, not boundary markers. It is a community of loving embrace; a wide-open community of people brought into existence to care for the very people whose similarity to us is trust in Jesus alone. God is not contained in Judaism, not siloed in Israel's narrow experience, just like God is not harnessed by any contemporary denomination, theology, nation, governmental system, or political party. God is at work among the Gentiles, Paul says, like it or not. If God is at work outside our lines, our lines are artificial.

We accept inclusion of other Christian denominations almost instinctively now, though we go through great pains to tease out the particulars of their errors. As sectarian as my tribe has been, the majority of members no longer worry about the eternal destination of Baptists or Methodists like I did when I was a kid. Some folks consider outsiders misguided, but not apostate. But that doesn't mean we aren't clinging to other lines. The lines now are theological and political.

Like John Piper wishing Rob Bell "farewell" over holding essentially the same view of hell as the much-celebrated C. S. Lewis, difference *must* become divisions.[1] Laura, and the folks using their Amazon Prime memberships to send Thomas Sewell books to my doorstep, couldn't conceive of a Christian who wasn't expressly a Republican. Since Richard Nixon's "Southern Strategy," Laura had been fed a steady diet of complaints about the "liberal media," how liberals supported lawlessness, and that liberalism was a "mental disorder." In her circle and against all evidence to the contrary, Barack Obama is an African-born, secret Muslim socialist, and all

---

1. Bell, *Love Wins*, 113.

Democrats were out to ruin the country by having abortions performed in the ladies bathroom at Target by a lesbian named Fantasia. Liberals wanted to send transgender men into the women's room to prey on little girls in their missionary quest to embed perversion into the soul of the country as they spit on the grave of Ronald Reagan. Evidence didn't matter. The pundits she listened to and the authors she read were so unanimous in their critique that that unanimity suggested truth. The religious leaders pumped into her home via Christian radio and paid airtime on Christian cable networks echoed the misinformation she already accepted as accurate. Laura never considered that her indignation was ginned-up by deliberate forces simply interested in building constituencies for television shows, news networks, and book sales. Laura is not bad nor evil, she is a victim of the discourse, a discourse that is unconcerned with Paul's vision of covenant in the New Testament.

It wasn't that Laura was conservative that made her reject others—most people I know are conservative. Her animus was bred from making a particular brand of conservatism an article of faith. For her, a particular orthodoxy concerning gay-marriage, Muslims, and a white-hot passion to overturn *Roe v. Wade* made someone a Christian, pure and simple. To draw breath without a stone-cold conviction that her issues weren't the paramount issues was anathema.

The same is true for many of my friends on the theological and political Left—though those categories don't always go together. They too are served a litany of images of conservatives being hate-filled, anti-intellectual, homophobic, war-mongering, sex-policing xenophobes. The orthodoxy on the Left is to critique, mock, denigrate, and marginalize their opponents to the point of social and political annihilation. For them, if you're not with us, then you're a backward, simple-minded red-neck whose views don't deserve a hearing in educated society. "Get back to us when you wriggle out of your primordial ooze," they say.

The same exterior forces are at work there too: a media (publishing, movies, television, and radio) hell bent, not on integrality, but on selling ideas and products for cultural domination. Christians, perhaps now like never before, suffer under demonic powers and principalities whose essential work is to stir and exploit disunity. The same powers and principalities will always give us a convenient scapegoat—immigrants, the 1 percent, Muslims, Liberals, Conservatives, Mexicans, corporations—anyone can serve as the receptacle for our vitriol as long as we don't notice the veiled hand of evil powers working the gears.

In August 2009, Alicia Sanchez lay down next to her Jeep Cherokee preparing to die. Her son, Carlos (6), had just recently died in a remote part of Death Valley National Park. After running out of gas and water, Alicia and her son walked more than ten miles in search of help but found none. After Alicia was found, she explained how she and Carlos had become lost in Death Valley. She made a wrong turn. She explained that she was merely following her GPS. Over a fifteen-year period at least a dozen people have died in Death Valley due to what many are beginning to call "death by GPS." Charlie Callagan, Death Valley wilderness coordinator, explains the phenomenon. "People are renting vehicles with GPS, and they have no idea how it works and they are willing to trust the GPS to lead them into the middle of nowhere." And this is what I mean by being a victim of the discourse. Christians aren't brainwashed, but many of us have become so dutifully committed to unshakably trusting partisan and divisive voices. Those same voices trust that we won't check the footnotes on their fallacies and that we will enact their falsely engineered angst against one another. These forces can only grow if we forget our shared story.

The Jews of Paul's day forgot their story. They had become victims of a Jewish interior world that envisioned God's salvation, not for a "large family" *including* Gentiles, but a smaller "large family" only including Jews. And why not? Like the church of my childhood, nearly everyone they loved and respected told them that exclusion was best for flourishing. But exclusion doesn't create flourishing.

The church Paul envisions calls believers to be an affront to every effort at disharmony. Philip Yancey puts it this way in *Vanishing Grace: Whatever Happened to the Good News?*: "When I read accounts of the New Testament church, no characteristic stands out more sharply than diversity, the primary testing ground of grace. Beginning with Pentecost—a gathering of people from many countries—the Christian church dismantled the barriers of gender, race, and social class that had marked Jewish congregations."

The Christian church is a bigger tent and larger family than many of us imagine. In his letters, Paul refers to Jesus as "our Lord" fifty-three times. Only once, in contrast, does the expression "my Lord," occur. That means the heart of the Christian church is sharing and commonality, what Christians call communion.

By kindergarten, I had become a three-foot anti-Christ, sitting in the corner, singing songs of worship while nurturing the schemes of Satan in my heart—schemes that demanded that walls and separation serve as vehicles for righteousness; schemes that allowed a few shrill, demanding, and demagogic voices to serve as my only resource for truth. The discourse trained me to blacklist people who were unlike me. If you've been a Christian for more than fifteen minutes, you've done the same. You've looked at another person and thought, "She's not *really* a Christian." You've had a "those people" moment when you've thought, "I'm not sure about 'those people.'" Or perhaps you've had a "real Christian" moment, when you've said, "'Real Christians' would never (fill in the blank)." Sometimes our "real Christian" moments are about lifestyle; other times they are about beliefs or a particular interpretation of Scripture. When we do this, most of us are not trying to be combative. We think we are doing the right thing, keeping faith genuine and undiluted. But we've been victimized by a false discourse, born out of disengagement with the New Testament vision of church.

I was a victim. Laura is a victim.
God's family is a large family!
It includes everyone.

5

Superiority Complex

Our true nationality is mankind.

—H. G. Wells

O UR 2015 FAMILY VACATION landed us at the National Civil Rights Museum at the Lorraine Motel in Memphis, Tennessee. Thankfully, my daughters are the kind of kids who don't have to be bribed or dragged to museums. One year, after complaining about the "lameness" of mom's and dad's vacations, we let them decide where to take our final end-of-summer trip. Our oldest, Malia, wanted to see the Magna Carta while it was still on exhibit at the Houston Museum of Natural Science, and our youngest daughter, Katharine, chose the Alamo in San Antonio. Apparently, we've developed a healthy sense of geek in our home, so a day spent at the National Civil Rights museum was right up our alley.

We arrived prepared. Both of my daughters read multiple books about the civil rights era. Malia focused on Martin Luther King Jr., but Katharine focused her attention on Rosa Parks—the brave, strategic NAACP worker who elected to stay seated when she was asked to stand up. Heading into the trip, I read Fred Gray's *Bus Ride to Justice*. Our clan was more than geared up to drink in the experience. The National Civil Rights Museum is a triumph! Beautiful, rich, informative, and stirring. So stirring, in fact, that the first two hours, for me, were a mix of depression, rage, and unexpected shame.

Life-sized statues of the enslaved brought to America from Africa jab visitors in the face with their horrible reality. You can see worried, pained, and sometimes broken expressions that convincingly capture the reality of these men and women, forced under penalty of death to row their own way into bondage. These men and women looked like me. They look like my daughters. The build of their bodies, their tight, curly hair are the same as mine. And unlike any time before in my life, I felt ashamed. Ashamed to be black. Ashamed that my ancestors were slaves and their children were survivors of being enslaved. I was instantly ashamed that, since my ancestors were black and their children were survivors of captivity, my grandfather never finished the third grade. I was ashamed that in my family, my father was the only son who managed to go to college—the trickle-down traces of an America designed to cast black and brown people as a permanent underclass. I was ashamed to be born in America and, frankly, to have to call myself an American. Within the first forty feet of this museum I was reminded that I live in a country where too few of her founders considered my ancestors real people, made in the image of God. They thought *they* were better than *us*, even while *we* were building America.

Strangely, America's enslavers built the nation's wealth on the backs of slaves and still managed to feel superior to their wealth-creating slaves for hundreds of years.

A full year before America declared her independence, the baseless superiority complex—and hypocrisy—of whites was already exposed. By 1775, enslavers carried 160,000 Africans to Chesapeake colonies, 140,000 to colonies in the Carolinas and Georgia, and 30,000 to northern colonies. What's more, these numbers fail to capture the untold regiment of enslaved Africans sent to sugar colonies. In 1775, the nation that proclaimed that all men were created equal boasted a population of 2.5 million people. Five hundred thousand of them were forced into violent, uncompensated, murderous servitude.

Two million cruel actors launched America's story with authorized barbarity. This is a fact of history. Pressing against every teaching of Jesus regarding the treatment of others and the explicit instructions of God regarding the treatment of foreigners (Lev 19:34; Deut 24:19–21), the darker-skinned were subjugated based solely on the darkness of that skin.

The great tragedy of America's racial tensions began when European Christians rejected the explicit teachings of Jesus (Matt 25:35) for economic gain. And it was for economic gain. According to Edward E. Baptist's book *The Half Has Never Been Told: Slavery and the Making of American Capitalism*, by 1850, enslaved Africans were worth $1.3 billion, a full one-fifth of America's wealth. Enslavement built America's economy.

Europeans fleeing one form of persecution came to the New World and enacted another form of persecution.

Yet even after the end of formal enslavement, the legacy of the enslavers birthed a regime of domestic terror. For example, in 1930 three African American teenagers—Tom Shipp, Abe Smith, and James Cameron—were accused of murder and rape in Indiana. Rather than standing trial, a mob of thousands gathered outside the city jail. The flock broke in, beat the boys to within an inch of life, lynched the trio, and stayed to pose for pictures.

Lynchings—as well as all violence perpetuated by the empowered upon the defenseless—were, and are, warnings. At the Indiana lynching, and many others like it, photographers were on hand to capture the experience to sell postcards. Men, women, and even children were frequently present. Photographs typically reveal one or more attendees pointing to the lifeless, swaying bodies of the murdered. There is no equality in these pictures. Neither perpetrators nor witnesses feared consequences for their felonies. The message was clear: Stay in your place or experience the same. The nation that threw off the shackles of tyranny triggered its own form of systemized oppression, murder, and savagery.

America—and many nations around the world—still endure the legacy of murder and savagery erected on the rickety scaffolding of racial and national superiority.

On August 8, 2011, just before sunrise, two carloads of white teens outside of Jackson, Mississippi, set out on a mission to find and hurt a black person. It didn't matter who. There was only one prerequisite: the victim had to be black. After a night of drinking, one kid said to the group, "Let's go mess with some niggers." Together, they found a potential victim in the parking lot of the Metro Inn on the outskirts of Jackson, Mississippi. James Craig Anderson, a forty-nine-year-old auto plant worker, was in the parking lot, attempting to get in his car. The group attacked Anderson, beat and robbed him. One witness reported hearing the group of teens shouting "white power" as they returned to the truck after the beating.

After returning to his truck, Deryl Dedmon Jr., an eighteen-year-old from Brandon, Mississippi, floored the gas of his green F250 pickup and ran down James Craig Anderson as the beaten man was stumbling away from the scene. He was killed instantly. A modern-day lynching.

James Craig Anderson was murdered seven miles from where I was born.

It would be easy to write off these acts, as some attempted, as the alcohol-fueled actions of youths gone wild. But they didn't set out to "mess" with *someone*. They wanted "some niggers." They had predetermined whose lives, whose bodies, were less valuable than their own. Dedmon and his friends didn't debate who their victim should be. This wasn't as impulsive as some might think. It was premeditated. They'd long ago decided which people were worthy of abuse. It was in their bones!

What would make people—regardless of color, socioeconomic status, or education—choose to visit bloodshed and fury on others? The same misguided passions that created American slavery, apartheid, and Jim Crow. Sadly, they are now on display through Islamic Fundamentalism, rape-culture, economic stratification, and continuing racism and sexism across the globe. For all the theories and questions we'd like to deploy to explain the corrosion inside the human heart, the reality is that our mistreatment of one another is just plain, vanilla superiority.

Because of our desire to find any lever that might prove us superior to others, and because superiority can only rip the seams of family and community, it can have no place in the church! In fact, as the church began the first Christians had to exterminate any notion of racial or national superiority before the virus could infect the body. For Christians, both then and now, to allow either open or disguised inklings of supremacy or dominance is to plant weeds in the soil of the gospel.

The difficulty, though, is that Jewish Christians had only experienced religion as a system built on superiority. As Jews, they were the people of God, superior to other people. The way they demonstrated this superiority wasn't through brutality, economic and educational inequality, or enslaving others. The way they displayed superiority was through what they called "works of Torah."

The problem Paul faces in his letters, particularly Romans, is the failed state of the Jewish people and the lack of efficacy in the "works of Torah" in which the Jews placed their hope. God's covenant with Israel was intended to deal with the problem of evil in the world. Israel was elected to be the remedy to Adam's sin, the light of the *entire* world. Instead they had chosen to be reflections of the darkness. Knowing this to be the case, the litany of sins in Romans 1 begins to make more sense.

Romans 1, besides laying out the theme of Romans—"I'm not ashamed of the good news; it's God's power, bringing salvation to everyone who believes—to the Jew first, and also equally, to the Greek"

(1:16)—also announces God's intent in salvation. Salvation is for both the Jews and Greeks.

This is shocking news if you are a Jew. It's appalling because you think you have kept up your end of the bargain. Your end is the practice of the "works of Torah"—circumcisions and other obvious boundary markers that separated Jews from Gentiles. These are the behaviors that demonstrated and marked you as God's people. The works of Torah didn't simply designate someone as *different* from others, or even justified before God. The "works of Torah" made Jews *better*. They were superior. Like Joseph's coat of many colors, the Torah revealed you as special among the rest of the Father's offspring. The crash landing Jews faced when accepting the good news of Jesus was that they were not better than Gentiles. That's what Paul means when he says he is "not ashamed." He is not ashamed that the God of the universe has fulfilled God's eternal plan to redeem all nations.

Too many Christians disregard the racial and national aspects of Paul's arguments, instead choosing to make claims about public professions of faith. Being "not ashamed of the good news" isn't about a teenager being willing to risk bringing her Bible to her public high school or saying a prayer at the prospect of being ridiculed. Neither is it primarily about our personal willingness to be associated with advocating Christian's perspectives in the market place. We live in a society where too many Christian people think Paul's "shame" is tantamount to our willingness to face public mockery, objection, or marginalization. It's not. Paul's concern is the default condition in the human heart that seeks supremacy over others and the scandalous news that God is working for the reconciliation of all people not against it.

We should applaud all those instances of courage when people graciously face actual persecution to gain a hearing for the gospel. But that barely brushes Paul's meaning. When Paul announces that he is "not ashamed" he intends his readers to reject the distorting belief that in God's mind some people are better than others.

I Wish I Knew Her Name

Perhaps my greatest offense was perpetrated in the eleventh grade. Though I was sixteen, I didn't have a car. I didn't even have a driver's license. That meant my mother drove me to school every morning. I could have taken the bus, but it was hot and crowded and loud, so I opted to have my mom drop me off at Stone Mountain High School on her way to work. I was there a full hour before school started. I was often the first student there and met the custodian as he was unlocking the school doors.

Arriving that early meant that most mornings I finished my homework while sitting in the cafeteria where all students spent the morning until the first bell rang at 8:00 a.m. Each morning, at 7:15, after I'd already delved into my leftover homework, a special bus arrived delivering a few of our Special Education students. There was one girl on the bus that I will never forget. We called her "Rat Girl."

I never knew, and probably didn't care, what her diagnosis was. She was mentally delayed, as well as suffering from some physical deformities. That's why we called her Rat Girl. She was African-American with short, braided hair that was always pulled back into a ponytail. The ponytail pulled her forehead and ears back in such a way that it mimicked the look of a rat. Add to that her long nose and "Rat Girl" was an easy invective, though not terribly creative. Her speech was slurred and she frequently had bits of saliva on the corners of her mouth. She was also very friendly.

Each morning, as I sat poring over my homework, she'd approach the other early arrivers, stretch out her hand and say, "Good morning." We were teenagers and none of us were comfortable with that level of difference between people, but we were also downright mean. The same events unfolded every morning. She would approach a student and say, "Good morning." They would stretch out their hand as if they were going to welcome her. And as their hands were about to touch, kids would shout "Ewwww!" and run away. After a while, some classmates would even begin to approach her first and perform the same degrading deed.

It was embarrassing and horrendous, and I just sat there.

I did more than sit there. Somewhere in my soul I prayed that she would never come to me, never say "good morning" to me. Just keep your head down, I told myself. Because in the curious world of adolescent hierarchy, to demonstrate anything close to support for those deemed outcasts or misfits meant risking the erosion of any reputation you may have scraped together in the eyes of your peers. High school reminded me of playing "King Of The Hill" as a boy. They elbow, push, kick, and pull to be on top never realizing that once you've made it, you're only standing on a pile of dirt.

Nothing could have been more inconceivable to those of us gathered in the cafeteria before school than the idea that Rat Girl (and gosh, do I wish I knew her name), was the same as us. We would have been embarrassed to be associated with her. The simple kindnesses of shaking her hand and returning her "good morning" would nudge us too close to ridicule, so we dared not attempt it. My high school friends knew I was a Christian. I knew more Bible than most and went to youth group and on summer mission trips, but by Paul's definition, I was "ashamed of the good news." Without thought, the cafeteria crew had come to believe that by virtue of birth—after all she was born different—they were somehow more worthy and valuable people.

That's what supremacy does. It tears the fabric of unity.

Two thousand years after the gospel invaded the world, what remains clear is that the insidious infection of superiority still infects Christians and the Christian church. Despite the aims of Paul, the church is ashamed of the gospel. We are ashamed of the gospel every time we harbor unity-destroying superiority in any way. It's always easy to feel superior to people whose lifestyles and beliefs differ from ours. It may be the religious or sexual Other; it might be political opposition, or the uneducated or underclass. Most of us feel superior to someone, never realizing that those perceptions of superiority are at cross-purposes with God.

Like white slave owners in America, apartheid's supporters in South Africa, and like too many men who oppress and suppress minorities, women, and the sexual Other today, the Jews had come to believe they had a divine right to superiority. And this shouldn't be missed. The Jews felt superior because they thought their Bible told them to feel superior. But Paul confronts them with a simple fact: They have no justification to feel justified.

Like all of us, Israel was infected with sin. Sin is a virus with no human cure. The darkness of our hearts and heads is universally shared and universally deleterious. What's more, we bask in the glory of sin and condone darkness when we see it in others. Later in Romans 1, Paul outlines, not every, but many of the sins we are capable of and routinely practice—injustice, wickedness, greed, envy, murder, enmity, deceit, cunning, arrogance, self-important boasting, disobedience to parents, shameful sexual acts, and others (1:26–31). It is simply pointless then to tease out one or two sins and behave as if the condemnation of God rests more heavily on some particular violations than on others, but we will come to that later. Paul's point is that God's people failed to be God's people, and that creates a problem. God must remain faithful to the covenant when God's partners haven't kept their end of the deal. N. T. Wright puts it this way: "If the covenant was put in place to deal with evil in the world, then the failure of the covenant people to be the light of the world means that the covenant itself seems to be under threat. . . . What is the covenant God to do about the failure of his covenant people (3:2) to be faithful, on their part, to this covenant?"[1]

God's answer is not to wait until the end of time and rescue Israel nor, as some supposed, to send a conquering Savior to thrust the Romans out of Jerusalem and establish a Holy Seat occupied by an earthly king from the line of David. God's answer is what it has always been: to rescue all people through Jesus's cross right now. This fact is still foolishness in a world dominated by domination. In a world inclined to marginalize the Other, God-followers continue to struggle with their desire for primacy. An all-embracing God embrace remains outrageous.

My wife and I experienced this recently during a months-long and odd exchange with an old college friend named Kyle. After college, Kyle went to work as a physician's assistant in Lubbock, Texas. Like Rochelle and I, Kyle was raised a faithful church member, with church life being the center of his upbringing. Kyle found himself in Lubbock and like all young people launching a career, he needed to stake out a new life and form new relationships. One of these relationships was with the doctor he worked for.

Introverted and socially awkward, Kyle often struggled to connect with others, especially peers. He is one of those guys who was born fifty years too late. His preferences were for the music, television, movies, clothing styles, and culture of his grandparent's world. These inclinations made relationships anxiety-producing and laborious for Kyle, so it was with incredible daring that Kyle stepped out to form a friendship with the doctor he worked for.

Soon, Kyle had a new friend. The two frequently lunched together, sharing stories of life and family and ambition. But all of that came to a crashing thud when Kyle learned his new friend was gay.

Kyle emailed me, brokenhearted about his new friend and asking what I thought he should do. He sounded perplexed. He wasn't. I could tell that nothing I said mattered. Kyle had already decided what he was going to do. At the end of the week, during their weekly Friday lunch, Kyle announced that he was glad to continue to work in the office, but "we can't be friends."

"Why?" the doctor asked.

1. Wright, "Romans and the Theology of Paul," 30–67.

"Because you're gay. I'm a Christian and Christians can't be friends with homosexuals."

That was it. That was all the reasoning Kyle gave, and all he felt he needed to give. He shared with me later his conviction that Christians can't be friends with people if they disagreed with their lifestyle. Kyle spent his entire life believing that Christians were superior to other people and that their superiority was birthed through a lifetime of checking the right boxes, crossing every T, holding the right beliefs, and, most of all, some level of religious performance. It's not that Kyle rejected grace, but that we really believed that grace had to be accompanied by some level of right doing and purity; keeping oneself as "undefiled by the world." To stay pure meant staying away from the impure unless it just couldn't be avoided.

All of his life Kyle attended church—even midweek services—and had been drenched in the Christian subculture. He read his Bible, was baptized, had Christian friends, and had even gone into a career designed to help people. He was, he thought, the dictionary definition of a Christian. But he was the dictionary definition of a Christian based on his own faithfulness rather than God's. Kyle had all the externalities and accouterments of Christianity, and those same trappings defined being a good person. When it came to homosexuals, Kyle was fine with taking a paycheck. He was not fine splitting the lunch check.

There was no evangelistic zeal here, no concern for destructive and ungodly behaviors as some might argue, just the hood and robe of superiority. Paul addresses this kind of merit-based salvation directly: "So is there any place left for boasting? No. It's been shut out completely. And how? By what sort of law? The law of works perhaps? No! By the law of faith. We hold that people are justified, that is, made right with God through faith, which has nothing to do with the deeds the law prescribes" (Rom 3:27–28 The Kingdom New Testament).

It would come as a shock to Kyle to discover, as the Jewish Christians in Rome did, that the behaviors he thinks demonstrate faithfulness to God actually tear apart the church. In fact, these behaviors are opposed to building beloved community. The break of table fellowship in exchange for judgment is the opposite of what the Bible shows us Jesus doing. World history is proof enough that thoughts of mental, emotional, natural, or physical superiority cut at the root of brotherhood and do not belong in the kingdom of God. To harbor them is to resist both community and Kingdom.

But to say that personal feelings of superiority alone are problematic still doesn't cut to the quick of what hinders beloved community. Feelings of personal superiority find sustainable company in feelings of ethnic and national superiority. For many in America, the notion of "American exceptionalism" (national superiority) is both demonstrably true and an unquestionable good.

In 2009, President Obama was questioned by Edward Luce of the *Financial Times* about American exceptionalism. The president's critics had come to see his willingness to engage countries like Iraq in diplomacy and seek deeper commitments to and from foreign allies as a kind of repudiation of the national prominence.

> Luce: [C]ould I ask you whether you subscribe, as many of your predecessors have, to the school of American exceptionalism that sees America as uniquely qualified to lead the world, or do you have a slightly different philosophy? And if so, would you be able to elaborate on it?
>
> Obama: I believe in American exceptionalism, just as I suspect that the Brits believe in British exceptionalism and the Greeks believe in Greek exceptionalism. I'm enormously proud of my country and its role and history in the world. If you think about the site of this summit and what it means, I don't think America should be embarrassed to see evidence of the sacrifices of our troops, the enormous amount of resources that were put into Europe postwar, and our leadership in crafting an Alliance that ultimately led to the unification of Europe. We should take great pride in that.
>
> And if you think of our current situation, the United States remains the largest economy in the world. We have unmatched military capability. And I think that we have a core set of values that are enshrined in our Constitution, in our body of law, in our democratic practices, in our belief in free speech and equality, that, though imperfect, are exceptional.
>
> Now, the fact that I am very proud of my country and I think that we've got a whole lot to offer the world does not lessen my interest in recognizing the value and wonderful qualities of other countries, or recognizing that we're not always going to be right, or that other people may have good ideas, or that in order for us to work collectively, all parties have to compromise and that includes us.
>
> And so I see no contradiction between believing that America has a continued extraordinary role in leading the world towards peace and prosperity and recognizing that that leadership is incumbent, depends on, our ability to create partnerships,

because we create partnerships because we can't solve these problems alone.[2]

In response, critics rightly decried Obama's "exceptionalism" as unexceptional. Writing in *New Republic*, James Kirchick, responded, "If all countries are 'exceptional,' then none are, and to claim otherwise robs the word, and the idea of American exceptionalism, of any meaning."[3] Later, Louisiana Governor Bobby Jindal squawked that the President "won't proudly proclaim American exceptionalism."[4] What was found wanting in Obama's statement was not that America was "good, wonderful, unmatched," and even "exceptional." He used all those words. What was absent was the notion that America is superior. What President Obama did not connote, and what some of us mean by "exceptional," is not exceptionalism, but *elitism*. In many ways, being exceptional is fine, perhaps even a necessary virtue in a world where mediocrity often oppresses. Elitism is altogether different.

President Obama's comments and the critique received serve us—not because I want to convince anyone of the worth of any politician or particular political party—but as an illustration of the "shameful" news Paul announced to the Jews: they weren't exceptional for the reasons and in the way they thought they were exceptional. Paul argues it this way:

> Listen, if you claim to be a Jew, count on the law, and boast in your relationship with God; if you know His will and can determine what is essential (because you have been instructed in the law); and if you stand convinced that you are chosen to be a guide to the blind, a light to those who live in darkness, a teacher of foolish wanderers and children, and have in the law what is essentially the form of knowledge and truth—then tell me, why don't you practice what you preach? If you are going to sermonize against stealing, then stop stealing. If you are going to teach others not to commit adultery, then be completely faithful to your spouse. If you hate idolatry, then stop robbing the temples! If you pride yourself in having God's law, then stop dishonoring God by failing to keep its teaching. Here's what it says: "Because of you, God's reputation is slandered by those outside the covenant." (Rom 2:17–24 The Voice)

2. News Conference by President Obama, 4/04/2009, https://www.whitehouse.gov/the-press-office/news-conference-president-obama-4042009.

3. Kirchick, "Squanderer in Chief."

4. Jindal, Fox News Interview, February 9, 2015.

In short, your own sin convicts you as common, not exceptional. And remember, Paul is not writing about individual moral failure, as we like to think, though it certainly includes that. The heart of the argument is that the people have failed. The nation has failed. It doesn't require everyone within a nation to partake in sin for the nation to be pronounced guilty.

Therefore, American churches, with our national history of slavery, segregation, civil rights injustices, and uneven dispersal of justice, should be the first community to stand in solidarity with others. We have sinned grievously and stand guilty, yet God has made a way for salvation—a way that overcomes our individual and collective sin. The hard part is the acknowledgment that God's way means letting go of our boasting.

> So is there any place left for boasting? No. It's been shut out completely. And how? By what sort of law? The law of works perhaps? No! By the law of faith. We hold that people are justified, that is, made right with God through faith, which has nothing to do with the deeds the law prescribes. Is God the God of the Jews only? If He created all things, then doesn't that make Him the God of all people? Jews and non-Jews, insiders and outsiders alike? Yes, He is also the God of all the outsiders. So since God is one, there is one way for Jews and outsiders, circumcised and uncircumcised, to be right with Him. That is the way of faith. So are we trying to use faith to abolish the law? Absolutely not! In fact, we now are free to uphold the law as God intended. (Rom 3:27–31 The Voice)

We are given hints that this has always been—as Paul says, that this is what "God intended." Thumbing through the gospels, the men and women who welcome baby Jesus into the world are our first sign that ethnic and national distinctions were feckless boundary markers of no use to God. Jesus is born among his family, but because there was no room in the guest/ upper room (*kataluma*), he is born among the family's animals, but among his family nonetheless. Barely out of the womb Jesus is visited by shepherds, largely understood to be the outcasts, dregs, and poorest in the community—the people no one preferred to be with, like Rat Girl. Soon afterward, the Lord is visited by Magi, middle-eastern stargazers searching for a King. Other characters in this tale include an elderly couple—Zechariah and Elizabeth, who had just had their own unlikely baby, and a gray-haired prophetess named Anna. Simeon, too, is part of the story: a man so close to death that after seeing Jesus, he simply wishes for its onset. If Hollywood or AM Radio were in charge of casting, this scene would never have happened. A cast this diverse wouldn't ring as realistic. There are too many different kinds of people anticipating and visiting Jesus.

But in the Jesus story, everyone's in the picture.

When Jesus is present, the entire world comes together. The first miracle Jesus does is bring people together. The Christ child releases us from the false, self-satisfying deception that superiority is a sufficient way to see humankind.

Christians answer Paul's rhetorical question, "Is there any place left for boasting?" (3:27) with a full-throated "absolutely not!" Regardless of who you are, where you were born, your religious merits, race, gender, or any other accident of history and demographics, boasting cannot cohere to Christlikeness. If the idea of losing your boasting fills you with despair, if you're uneasy to learn that you are equal to all the people you've spent a lifetime hating, despising, or feeling superior to, what you're actually feeling is "ashamed of the gospel."

6

A Space for Grace

The story goes that a public sinner was excommunicated and forbidden entry to the church. He took his woes to God. "They won't let me in, Lord, because I am a sinner."

"What are you complaining about?" said God. "They won't let Me in either."

—Brennan Manning

THE CHURCH HAS ALWAYS been the metronome of my heart. I am a church kid—the southern, conservative kind of church kid in particular. No one would be surprised if you told them my mother gave birth to me inside a baptistry.

Church was my life, and it came as no surprise to many people when I chose the pastorate for a career. As a college freshman I gave a brief devotional thought during communion on a retreat for junior high students. When I was done, a woman named Dena who had taught my Bible class since I was in ninth grade leaned over to me and said, "You should be a preacher."

Like I said, I am a church kid. I'd have difficulty understanding myself outside of that context. I can't remember a time when the rhythm of church life wasn't in sync with the rhythm of my life. To some people's surprise, my wife, Rochelle, and I made sure we went to church while on our honeymoon. It was Wednesday night church too! Never did the cadence of church feel forced or awkward, it is just who I am. While in the flow of church life, I came to know the Bible and to understand, to varying degrees, what I believed God was up to in the world. I knew, from very early on, what sin was and why it was dangerous. The windows of church gave me a view into other people's lives. As a child I saw how divorce shredded families and what poor fathers and mothers and abusive husbands looked like. I knew husbands who cheated on their wives and college kids hooked on drugs. Rubbing against the lives of other people allowed me to see first hand why it was in my best interest to remain chaste until marriage and faithful once in. Sin is destructive, and I appreciated the pain I'd seen others endure. I had front row seats to other people's sins. I'm glad I did. In church, I learned what I wanted from life and wanted to avoid.

What I learned far less about is grace.

Touches of Grace

I cannot recall grace ever being a topic of conversation. We didn't talk about it at home. We didn't talk about it at church. I knew which church was the right one (mine!) because it had been explicitly stated time and again. I never had to hunt and peck for Scriptures to defend my worldview or our church practices. All that had been made more than clear. I knew what someone needed to do to be saved. The words from our church's favored hymns were downloaded in my mental hard drive, always available for quick access. All I can conclude is that I never heard about grace because we never talked about grace. And we never talked about grace for the same reason other topics are skimmed over or completely missed: We didn't think it was important!

This is the risk all church kids face. Because we've never known life without some glimmer of God, we only graze the magnitude of grace. When we're honest with ourselves we admit that we brush past grace because we think we only need it in meager doses. As Marilyn Monroe said, "I am good, but not an angel. I do sin, but I am not the devil." We know we're not "good," but we're "good" enough not to be "bad." Sure, we need a little grace for assurance against damnation because we looked at *Playboy* in high school or watched too much late-night Cinemax. Perhaps, we curse too much or short our tithe. We might even admit to taking a puff off a joint in college, or maybe we routinely lie in business deals to gain an advantage for the company, but we really aren't *that* bad. We lie to ourselves about our own goodness because there are some people who are *that* bad. But that *that* is the problem. It's a comparison game. And it's a rigged game! It's a game designed to let us come out on top. The *really* bad people are consistently the people we don't like or feel repelled or disgusted by. They are the folks who do the worst sins. But we're pretty selective about what "worst" means. Worst means homosexuals, Wall Street brokers, and hedge-fund managers. The worst are those who mistreat the poor, spousal abusers, Atheists, transgender men and women, folks from other religions or people inside our own religion who disagree about rather microscopic theological differences. The worst sinners can be anyone who raises our ire on any particular day. Evil always has a way of existing outside of ourselves.

Dr. Richard Beck introduces his book *Unclean* describing Paul Rozin's Dixie cup research and asking, "Imagine spitting into a Dixie cup. After doing so, how would you feel if you were asked to drink the contents of the cup?"[1] A year before Beck published *Unclean* I saw him perform Rozin's experiment live with college freshman. He asked two young women to spit into a Dixie cup and then drink their own spit. It was all pretty simple, spit and sip. These young women seemed representative of the group. If he'd picked the wrong type of freshmen boy, he may have gulped down the spit in some misguided attempt to prove his manliness in front of his peers—leaving them to wonder why, over the next few months, freshmen girls rejected his advances. The girls, however, weren't interested in swallowing the spit, even though it was their own; even though the spit had only recently evacuated their mouths. Nothing about the saliva changed except its location.

Dr. Beck wasn't shocked by their response. He knew Rozin's research. True to form, the young women did as most of us would do. Beck writes,

> Few of us feel disgust swallowing the saliva within our mouths. We do it all the time. But the second the saliva is expelled from the body it becomes something foreign and alien. It is no longer saliva—it is *spit*. Consequently, although there seems to be little *physical* difference between swallowing saliva in your mouth versus spitting it out and quickly drinking it, there is a psychological difference between the two acts. . . . We don't mind swallowing what is on the "inside." But we are disgusted by swallowing something that is "outside," even if that something was on the "inside" only a second ago.[2]

The spit, once outside the body, becomes a boundary line we are disgusted to cross. All us live with a visible boundary—our bodies—which forms an invisible shield—our *selves*. The best way to think about a "self" is

---

1. Beck, *Unclean*, 1.
2. Ibid., 2.

the physical, mental, emotional, and spiritual dimensions of you that make you "you." The self is what we think of when friends ask, "How are you doing?" When asked, we are most likely to answer, "How are you?" in a compartmental way. We might answer regarding our "spiritual life," or how we are doing "physically." Though it's problematic to divide spiritual life from the rest of life, we tend to think of ourselves in fragmented terms. What Beck points us to is the reality that when something, like spit or sin, is no longer part of our "self" it becomes foreign to the point of revulsion. We evaluate the external, even though it may be essentially the same, as foreign. In the end, other people's sins are *sins* while our sins are *mistakes*.

During the run-up to the 2016 presidential election, Donald Trump, who was running for the Republican nomination, was asked about his faith. Trump had been divorced multiple times, was previously featured on the cover of *Playboy* alongside a porn star, was also the owner of multiple casinos and strip clubs, and a frequent guest on *The Howard Stern Show* where he openly discussed sex acts and his marital infidelities. It seemed a reasonable question for someone vying for the support of American Evangelicals to answer. Trump responded, "People are so shocked when they find . . . out I am Protestant. I am Presbyterian. And I go to church and I love God and I love my church." Curious, interviewer and Republican pollster Frank Luntz probed further into Trump's beliefs, asking if he'd ever asked God for forgiveness. Trump replied, "I am not sure I have. I just go on and try to do a better job from there. I don't think so," he said. "I think if I do something wrong, I think, I just try and make it right. I don't bring God into that picture. I don't. When I drink my little wine—which is about the only wine I drink—and have my little cracker, I guess that is a form of asking for forgiveness, and I do that as often as possible because I feel cleansed," he said. "I think in terms of 'let's go on and let's make it right.'"[3]

Though Trump was thumped for it in some media circles and among those Christians opposed to his candidacy, what he said is fairly accurate to how we live. Our sins aren't really that bad because most of us believe we are good people. We're okay swallowing the saliva in our mouths.

Growing up in the church, I was taught to be a good person, which meant a kind of undiluted morality by which I would never need God's grace or, if finding myself deficient, would need very little to get me over the line. This feeling was echoed in a conversation I had with my friend Theodore, who like me, was raised in a Christian home and church but

3. Scott, "Trump Believes in God, but Hasn't Sought Forgiveness."

later left it to become Mormon. Over coffee, he explained to me that he thought grace was a great idea. "We all need grace," he told me, "but, it's just not enough. You need something else to get you over the finish line." Donald Trump's and Theodore's statements share a fundamental aversion to grace—at least their own personal need for grace. What makes more moral sense is hard work. I doubt they're alone in that assumption. Many people I know, especially those raised in America where the values of meritocracy and personal worthiness are embedded in the culture, find an institution rooted in grace to be virtue-less.

Could it be that grace strikes a blow to the heart of what we love more, the idea that our industry is what makes us valuable?

"There but for the grace of God go I" is a popular statement that hardly anyone believes. In fact, most people, especially those who consider themselves "successful," believe the direct opposite. Consider the way American Christians think about luck and success. They (or we) are successful because of the sweat of our own brow, our hard work and effort, and self-determination to press through obstacles, gain the credentials, and out work and out hustle others. Robert H. Frank gives us an inside look at our thinking in a May 2016 researched-based article in *The Atlantic*, "Why Luck Matters More than You Think." In short, "successful" people attribute their success to themselves:

> According to the Pew Research Center, people in higher income brackets are much more likely than those with lower incomes to say that individuals get rich primarily because they work hard. Other surveys bear this out: Wealthy people overwhelmingly attribute their own success to hard work rather than to factors like luck or being in the right place at the right time.
>
> That's troubling, because a growing body of evidence suggests that seeing ourselves as self-made—rather than as talented, hardworking, and lucky—leads us to be less generous and public-spirited. It may even make the lucky less likely to support the conditions (such as high-quality public infrastructure and education) that made their own success possible.[4]

"Successful" people are more likely to think highly of themselves and less likely to be public-spirited. Since their work accounts for success, then

---

4. Frank, "Why Luck Matters More than You Might Think."

work and success are inextricably tied together and any sharing of their wealth should stay with them or their kids.[5]

However, when asked by researchers to reflect on the events of their lives, the same people who credited their success to their work embraced something they had previously overlooked: luck. As reflection on life's actual circumstances occurred—parentage, financial resources, education levels of parents, school, social and familial connections, summer internships and jobs attained through those connections, etc.—the same subjects realized they'd been what researchers called "lucky." They attained opportunities, positions, funds, and other products, services, and goods they did not have to work for. At the very least they realized they didn't have to work as diligently as others without those same advantages. These realizations only came after they were forced to think of the actual events. Their unexamined instincts naturally overestimated their own contributions. But what Robert Frank calls "luck" is a secularized word for grace, a gift we receive without regard for our merit.

What can we learn from Beck and Rozin and Robert H. Frank? As humans, we are inclined to believe better of ourselves than what is actually true. Rozin's Dixie Cup and Robert H. Frank's research into success demonstrates that not only do we think more highly of ourselves than we ought, but that very thinking tempts us to think more lowly of others. The disgust we feel when something is outside of us, plus Donald Trump's desire to "make it right," plus Theodore's belief that we need something to "get over the finish line," and the assumption that success is built on work rather than luck, all conspire to distort or dismiss grace. We've never done anything *that* bad because we're basically good.

For children of the church like me, the great danger is that a distorted grace leads us away from grace dependence. But perhaps worse, like the subjects researched by Frank, a gnarled understanding of grace dependence leads us to be stingy about forgiveness for others. Down deep, for too many of us, grace seems like a get-out-of-jail-free card and if we go around handing it out like candy to children, how are people ever going to act rightly?

But that's the problem Wes and Nicole spotted in the church. Churches talk a good game about sin and welcome. We just don't practice it well. When opportunities for grace emerged, the Christians in front of Wes and Nicole chose repudiation instead. As we've seen, our tendency to be stingy

---

5. Thompson, "Rich People Are Great at Spending Money to Make Their Kids Rich, Too."

about grace isn't born of malevolence. It's born from elevated self-appraisal, the virus for which nearly all church folks will someday need an inoculation.

When the Apostle Paul looks at the early church, he knows all too well this temptation and it's capacity to sabotage Jesus's vision. When writing the letter to the church in Philippi, Paul—hoping to set the example for others—renounces his previously high self-evaluation, saying,

> If any try to throw around their pedigrees to you, remember my résumé—which is more impressive than theirs. I was circumcised on the eighth day—as the law prescribes—born of the nation of Israel, descended from the tribe of Benjamin. I am a Hebrew born of Hebrews; I have observed the law according to the strict piety of the Pharisees, separate from those embracing a less rigorous kind of Judaism. Zealous? Yes. I ruthlessly pursued and persecuted the church. And when it comes to the righteousness required by the law, my record is spotless.
>
> But whatever I used to count as my greatest accomplishments, I've written them off as a loss because of the Anointed One. And more so, I now realize that all I gained and thought was important was nothing but yesterday's garbage compared to knowing the Anointed Jesus my Lord. For Him I have thrown everything aside—it's nothing but a pile of waste—so that I may gain Him. When it counts, I want to be found belonging to Him, not clinging to my own righteousness based on law, but actively relying on the faithfulness of the Anointed One. This is true righteousness, supplied by God, acquired by faith (Phil 3:4–9 The Voice).

Why is this important? It's important because Paul shows us that receiving grace isn't something we simply do by accepting grace. It's not like a birthday present that you simply receive, say thanks, and enjoy. The first stage of grace isn't acceptance. It's rejection! The rejection of who we believe we are, who we've tried to show the world we are, and all that we have previously placed our trust in. Grace begins with the rejection of what the spiritual teachers call the "false self."

The false self is how we define ourselves when we fail to embrace our deeper identity as daughters and sons of God. The false self is our ego. The ego is defined by what David Brooks calls résumé virtues. The false self is obsessed with our position in the pecking order or hierarchy on the totem poll. It concerns itself with what we think we have achieved, what we're worth, what we've earned, and what we've accomplished. How can you recognize the false self? The teenager, or worse, the forty-five-year-old concerned about clothing labels or car models are living out of their false selves. The gym rat more concerned with perfect pecs rather than a healthy heart is eaten up with dishonesty about himself or herself. We can trust we are living from our false self when we are injured by every perceived slight and feel retaliatory whenever our feelings are hurt. At our worst, the false self divides the world. The great temptation of the false self is that it fools us into believing that life is fundamentally about self.

Grace, in its subtly beautiful way, lifts us beyond both our false self and our whole selves. All that we count as precious has been overwhelmed by the loving grace of Jesus. Rejection of our selves is the only means by which we die to Jesus rather than adding Jesus to our sterling résumés. In Philippians 4, Paul is doing more than recounting his biography. He is setting an example that should be normal for Christians: Reject all you were before by embracing the faithfulness of Jesus.

Given all that we said about Judaism and its relationship with the works of Torah, you can see why this might be upsetting to Jews. While acts of righteousness didn't provide salvation, they were evidence of it. Paul is turning the conventional knowledge on its head.

Frankly, Paul has an advantage over his readers. On his way to persecute followers of The Way, Paul is knocked off his horse, blinded, and given a new vision of faithful service by Jesus on the road to Damascus. Having that kind of experience is enough to get most of us to straighten up, fly right, and shake us into a new way of thinking and behaving.

It's a tougher pill to swallow, especially for all us church kids, to see necessary spiritual changes in the absence of a phenomenal event. We saw our high school friends drink themselves into near comas and our college friends find willing sexual playmates to fumble around with in the backseat of late-model cars. While we were off doing things the right way, we took note of those who didn't. There is a part of church kids that relishes when people get their comeuppance. "Play with fire, expect to get burned," our hearts quietly whisper. Lurking in the recesses of almost every church kid is an undercover Pharisee. When the bottom falls out for those who have failed to walk the straight and narrow, though we like to think of ourselves as loving people, we ask, "What did you expect?"

But then Paul blinds us with the same light that blinded him. As Paul continues to paint his picture of beloved community to the Christians in Rome, he writes, "But now for the good news: God's restorative justice has entered the world, independent of the law. Both the law and the prophets told us this day would come. This redeeming justice comes through the faithfulness of Jesus, the Anointed One, the Liberating King, who makes salvation a reality for all who believe—without the slightest partiality. You see, all have sinned, and all their futile attempts to reach God in His glory fail" (Rom 3:21–23 The Voice).

When I was a graduate student at Fuller Seminary in Northern California, a gentle, brilliant, older man named John was my professor. As we learned vocabulary and grammar, John chose the Greek word πᾶς (pas) as our declension adjective (the adjective you learn to understand how other adjectives work). I repeated "πᾶς, πᾶσα, πᾶν, πάντα" and its other declensions so often I began to hear it in my sleep. What's more, after I'd learned the declensions that well, I began seeing it everywhere in the New Testament. Though it's a little word, it's wrapped in beauty. "Pas" means all or every. It's used in the New Testament 1,243 times. One of those times is here in Romans 3. At the heart of the redemptive message of God is a great big "all." All have sinned and fall short of the glory of God, Paul urges.

Wouldn't it be great to live like grace was for *all* all the time? There are occasions when we cling to grace with desperation and everything within us, but there are other times when the idea of grace for all doesn't come as easily.

In early 1997, the biggest story in the country was Bill Clinton and Monica Lewinsky. You couldn't escape it. I was working for a church in south Texas at the time and when I'd go home for lunch, the White House daily press briefing was on television. It seemed like you couldn't go two hours without hearing the names Vernon Jordan, Ken Starr, and Linda Tripp. Saturday Night Live had a field day. Tons of books were written and parents were forced to talk to their children about sexual jargon and sex acts that they did not yet want to talk to their children about. Christians on one side of the political aisle condemned Clinton as unfit for office, and the president was publicly eviscerated for his behavior. But Christians on the other side of the aisle jumped up to say, "Don't you remember King David? He was a man after God's heart," and "that all have sinned and fallen short of the glory of God." While I'm sure everyone still has their own opinions about Bill Clinton, what was apparent on both sides of the aisle is that much of the reaction to Clinton's sins were based on pre-existing sympathies.

People who did not support President Clinton had zero grace. Those who supported him had plenty.

The same was true of Mark Sanford, the Republican governor of South Carolina, who said he went hiking in the Appalachians but really trekked down to Argentina to visit his mistress. The same people who supported Clinton chastised Sanford and the same people who criticized Clinton later nominated Sanford when he ran for House of Representatives.

Grace was allocated (or not) based on allegiances that were already in place. In my lifetime the same phenomenon has occurred with all kinds of populations in the church. When I was a young boy churches would distance themselves from people who were divorced or from teen moms, for example, but then something happened: preachers' and elders' children started getting divorced. Pregnant teenagers started to be the sons and daughters of church leaders, and all that distance that we mindlessly put between us and others suddenly wasn't so distant.

All that we've talked about leads us to a startling conclusion about grace: We base the receiving and giving of grace on how we *feel*. Paul wants to give us a new standard for both receiving and giving grace: All.

When church kids lose the "all," grace becomes muted at best and imperceptible at worst.

Grace Dispensers

John's e-mail landed in my inbox when I least expected it. For the life of me, I could not remember who he was but he remembered me. As he told me about himself, he relieved my anxiety about not remembering who he was. John told me that when I knew him, I knew him as Joan.

At the time, John was in the early process of gender confirmation and had already begun to live his life as a woman. His coworkers knew him as Joan and so did everyone s/he encountered when s/he started visiting and later attending our church as Joan.

Joan was tall and husky, but not so much so that you would immediately identify her as a man in transition. John went on to tell me about where s/he was with God, about changes he had made, and other areas where he struggled. Years earlier when we met, s/he had recently left his wife and three daughters. S/he believed he was born a mistake, a woman in a man's body (his words, not mine), and had decided to undergo gender-confirmation surgery. John shared with me the difficult season he was in as he came to church each week and tried to figure out what he did and did not want. His e-mail was short and to the point without a lot of fanfare.

He wanted to let me know that after several years of struggle he returned to his family, recommitted to his wife, and through a lot of forgiveness and therapy they were rebuilding their family and lives together. But most of all, John wanted to tell me that for the first time in fifty years, because of the way Joan was treated when she worshipped at our church, he experienced grace. When other Christians had run her off, she was welcomed into a simple, loving community of Jesus followers who had long ago decided that everyone would be invited "in" and there was no "out" when it came to God's community.

The church, at her best, dispenses grace. The church is not centered on morality nor theology. At her best, the church creates and nurtures the space for grace. Grace for all!

7

It's Clear to Me Now

Not everything that is faced can be changed, but nothing
can be changed until it is faced.

—James Baldwin

I NEARLY ABANDONED *THE MOTH* podcasts after listening to two episodes.
Because I'm a podcast junkie, my Monday morning begins with popping
open the podcast app on my iPhone and downloading the latest episodes of
more podcasts than I can possibly hope to listen to. When you subscribe to
as many podcasts as I do, you have to vet which gets listened to first, which
can wait, and which ones were good for a few episodes but couldn't keep
your attention. If the sound quality is poor, the length longer than my run,
or the content too flat, I'll make it through a few episodes before abandon-
ing the show for something more interesting. *The Moth* is a series of true
stories told by the storytellers that lived them. I thought I was listening to
my last episode of the show when I heard Hasan Minhaj. If Hasan's name
does not sound familiar to you, his face might. For several seasons he was
a correspondent on Comedy Central's *The Daily Show with Jon Stewart* and
was the star of his YouTube series, *The Truth*. Hasan was raised in California
after his parents immigrated to America from India. During his senior year
of high school, like most American teenagers, Hasan had to navigate prom.

Hasan actually did not want to attend prom and neither did the majority of his friends. School was about academics. Navigating social life,
fun, and extracurricular activities were unnecessary additions. Certainly,
dating wasn't on his agenda. Hasan's parents were strict and uninterested in
their son developing a social life. "My dad's rules were very simple growing

up: no fun, no friends, no girlfriends—you can have fun in med school,"
Hasan says. That was the plan. No fun. And no fun included prom.

But Hasan's AP calculus teacher, Mr. Davies, had other plans. Hasan
says, "One day he gets up in front of the entire class and goes, 'Alright, you're
all killing it academically, but I want you to know there's more to life than
just getting into U.C. Berkeley . . . I want you guys to live a life worth talking
about. Which is why I'm making it mandatory for everyone in this class to
go to prom.'" Hasan thought, "there's no way he's getting this group of social
misfits to prom." Knowing his students lacked the social confidence and
graces needed to extend or accept an invitation to prom, Davies set up a
March Madness type bracket to pair the students together. Initially, Hasan
thought the brackets were non-starters but as the weeks passed more and
more students were extending and accepting prom invites. It was all happening. Just a few days before prom, Mr. Davies walked to the board and
pulled down two more names, Hasan and his classmate Bethany. They were
a pair. Mr. Davies made it easy and Hasan wanted to go to prom regardless
of his father's wishes.

Since he didn't have permission from his father to date Bethany, the
two designed a plan. Hasan would retire to his room (which was relatively
normal), get dressed, exit through his window, ride his bicycle to Bethany's
house, and the two of them would take her father's car to prom. If he got
caught, he got caught, but he wanted this prom. In fact, in the few days
leading up to the dance, Hasan spent several nights with Bethany at her
home having dinner with her and her parents. They seemed to like him.
This eased Hasan's angst that this middle-class white family might find his
ethnicity objectionable.

When prom night came, everything went according to plan. Hasan
went to his room, put on his suit, doused himself in Michael Jordan cologne,
escaped through the window, and peddled his way over to Bethany's. If
you're like me, you're thinking this is all very *Napoleon Dynamite*. But when
Hasan arrived at Bethany's house, the plan's wheels fell off. As Bethany's
mom, Mrs. Reed, opened the door, her faced became flush with concern.
Over her shoulder, Hasan could see his fellow classmate, Jeff Berk, putting
a corsage on Bethany's wrist. Mrs. Reed looked at Hasan, saying, "Oh my
God, honey, Bethany didn't tell you? We think you're great, we really love
having you over, but . . . we're going to be taking a lot of pictures tonight . . .
and, um, we just don't think it'd be a good fit. Do you need a ride home? Mr.
Reed can give you a ride home."

Embarrassed, and feeling foolish, Hasan told her that he had his bike and didn't need a ride. He cycled his way home, climbed back through his window, and spent the night playing *Mario Kart*. Hasan says, "That's the nicest I've ever been dressed playing *Mario Kart*."

Vindicated God

Almost before the Christian church could walk there was a crippling tension. As we've seen earlier, it's the tension of bringing two peoples—Jews and Gentiles—together under the banner of Jesus. Folks who read the Bible and skip over this central issue perform a disservice to the Bible, the church, and to the suffering incurred by countless men and women. Just because we often find open discussion of racial and religious issues unpleasant doesn't mean those issues aren't real. The first disciples, Paul, and the early church mothers and fathers could not avoid the reality of the racial and religious differences obviously driving a wedge between them. In the twenty-first century, we simply see embracing Jesus as Lord as a kind of moral or lifestyle change, with little to no social or cultural repentance or transformation. But it was much more to them. It was a shift in both cultural and religious identity. When we read through the biblical texts, it's clear that each nation had their own local and regional deities. As Daniel, Shadrach, Meshach, and Abednego discovered, to live under the governing rule of another country was to face the prospect of receiving and worshipping that region's god(s) as *the* God. That was their world and it made sense. Imagine, if your god was the real god or the most powerful god, your country would not have fallen to our country. Every country had their own god(s). This is why the God of Israel, YHWH, was displeased when Israel's rulers, such as Solomon (Neh 13), married foreign women. What YHWH found sinful was not that these women were from other races, but there was a tacit, and sometimes overt, assumption that to marry foreign women meant incorporating foreign gods into Israel. Foreign wives meant foreign allegiances, and as the Law of Moses stated, Israel was to have "no other gods."

So when Israel's God, through the death and resurrection of Jesus, is vindicated as the *only* Lord, YHWH is no longer a regional deity. Israel's God has been proven to be the true God. The long-held beliefs about how gods function is overturned. Israel's God has been revealed to be everyone's God. But human beings have always had a difficult time changing their minds on a dime, especially when it comes to race and religion. Once you've considered someone as vile, reprehensible, sub-human, or unlovable, it's not easy to turn the page. Vices like hate, anger, and disdain don't emerge overnight and can't be eradicated by a new mental understanding of personhood, no matter how hard we try. Many of us dislike the same people groups we disliked as children or still carry the prejudices that were handed down to us by family members and close friends, even though we long ago first tried to disassemble them intellectually. Perhaps one of the reasons so much tension exists in the church regarding issues of hospitality and acceptance isn't because Christians are homophobic or racist or xenophobic. Perhaps the deeper issue is that "we just don't think it'll be a good fit." This, it seems, is what happened to the Apostle Peter and what continues to happen in some Christian communities.

The Continuing Conversion of Peter

Peter might be the most up-and-down character in the New Testament. He walks on water with Jesus, but fails, yet he's the only disciple who walks on water. Peter is the first to confess Jesus as Lord, but he also denies Jesus three times on the night the Lord was betrayed. Peter races to the empty tomb on Easter morning, gives the inaugural sermon of the church on Pentecost Sunday, and is the primary character for the first half of the book of Acts. Throughout his lifetime, Peter is a pendulum of getting it right, getting it wrong, and getting it right again. Peter constantly failing and constantly recalculating after failure makes him one of the more lovable people in Scripture. In his deficiencies Peter is very human, which is good news for us. One area where Peter repeatedly implodes is with whom he wants to take a picture. Peter is not a bad person. He is not evil. He, like most of us, is constantly inconsistent. Peter's biggest concern, like many Christians, is that he "does not have in mind the concerns of God, but merely human concerns" (Matt 16:23).

What are human concerns? Human concerns revolve around the false self and ego. They consist of saving face and comporting the self to popular social, political, and financial norms and the mainstream ways of thinking and acting. Human concerns typically center on what we think will help us gain and hold esteem in human eyes. Human concerns ask questions like, "Who else is coming to the party? Does this make me look fat? How can I win in even meaningless endeavors?" Human concerns allowed Bethany

Reed's parents to wound Hasan. They weren't concerned about a human; they were concerned about human concerns. Those are different concerns.

Much of Peter's life is given to human concerns, so God creates an opportunity to shake him from his obsession with optics for good. God arranges a meeting for Peter with a God-fearing man named Cornelius. The problem was that Cornelius isn't only a God-fearing man, but he is also a Gentile. This meeting pinches every nerve in Peter's body about who Gentiles were in God's eyes.

In Acts 10 God sends an angel (literally: messenger) to Cornelius, but this is how Acts first introduces us to Cornelius: "Cornelius, a Roman Centurion and a member of a unit called the Italian Cohort, lived in Caesarea. Cornelius was an outsider, but he was a devout man—a God-fearing fellow with a God-fearing family. He consistently and generously gave to the poor, and he practiced constant prayer to God. About three o'clock one afternoon, he had a vision of a messenger of God" (Acts 10:1–3 The Voice). Cornelius is not just *some* Gentile. He is a God-fearing Gentile with a God-fearing family. He is what attorneys call a "perfect plaintiff," a man whose life is without reproach and hard to criticize. God has something to teach Peter, but he's not going to make it easy. Cornelius is also a *Roman* Centurion, not only a man of power, but a contributor in the government that crucified Jesus. The messenger instructs Cornelius to send for Peter, which is exactly what Cornelius does.

Just as Cornelius is beginning to obey his instructions, God sends a message to Peter, in the form of a dream. "About noon the next day, as they were on their journey and approaching the city, Peter went up on the roof to pray. He became hungry and wanted something to eat; and while it was being prepared, he fell into a trance. He saw the heaven opened and something like a large sheet coming down, being lowered to the ground by its four corners. In it were all kinds of four-footed creatures and reptiles and birds of the air. Then he heard a voice saying, 'Get up, Peter; kill and eat'" (Acts 10:9–13). Unlike Cornelius, Peter objects: "By no means, Lord; for I have never eaten anything that is profane or unclean" (Acts 10:14). The die has already been cast in this story: Cornelius—the outsider—is eager to follow God's instruction, while Peter—the insider—demurs.

Every time I read Acts 10 I'm reminded of Rat Girl. I'm also reminded of a boy named Scott who moved from Texas to Georgia my senior year of high school. There may not be many things more socially cruel than a parent moving a child entering their last year of high school, but his parents did. Scott played the trumpet and joined my close friends and me in both the marching band and our highly touted jazz band. Since we had been the best jazz band in the state for more than twenty years and had toured Europe, playing at the best, most highly attended festivals there, we all thought we were special. Even though anyone could sign up, we all thought you needed to earn your way in "our" jazz band. Having just ridden in from Texas, there's no way Scott could have earned his way in.

We treated Scott like trash. We mocked his boots and his slight touch of Texas drawl. He wore a belt buckle larger than a hubcap, and we were merciless. Since he spoke with a piddling lisp we intimated that he was gay. I knew to treat people better. I just didn't. I was a faithful churchgoer and Christian. But like all adolescents, I figured if they're making fun of him, they're not making fun of me. That was a stupid way of thinking. I was an insider. I was a senior. Drum major. I conducted rehearsals and was popular in the small tribe that is band kids. Looking back on it now, I had more cache and influence with those hundred or so students than almost anyone. I wasn't made fun of in that group, and there was little risk that I would be. There was simply no risk for me to tell others to lay off, but I didn't do it. I was more than an insider. I was the ultimate insider! I wasn't completely without conscience, though. I experienced pangs in my soul as my friends mistreated Scott. Even late into the school year after enduring our daily torments, Scott stuck around. I never said anything or did anything, not because I was a kid and didn't know any better, but because I didn't want Scott's Otherness to tarnish my In-ness.

I was not so different from the Reeds. My friends and I, like many people, had come to believe in an invisible, but powerful force: group identity. Group identity—or what some sociologists call "collective identity"—is the shared sense of belonging to a group based on identifying markers, or boundary markers. Boundary markers are highly visible but relatively superficial traits or practices. Sociologists tell us that you and I make a great many decisions not in light of what we think, feel, and believe, but what we think the group thinks we ought to think. Why? Because boundary markers are terribly useful psychologically. Imagine moving to a new town or taking a new job. We can't possibly meet everyone. Life is too busy to spend time discovering who the smartest, funniest, and most insightful people are. We thoughtlessly gravitate to the people who are *visibly* most like us. Boundary markers allow us to get a quick read. They also allow us to prejudge someone before we invest time getting to know them.

Ever wonder why there are black churches and white churches? Part of it is our boundary markers. Ever wonder why, when something happens in the news, you know what Democrats are going to say, or what Republicans are going to say before they say it? Boundary markers are at play. Boundary markers let us know who's in and who's out, before we have to think about it. We like the idea of people being judged by the content of their character, but what we do in practice is judge one another on highly visible, relatively superficial traits or practices. You and I are what sociologists call "cognitive misers." Simply put, we categorize people because it saves time and mental and emotional energy. It's too hard to know and understand people, so we save ourselves the trouble by stereotyping. Being a cognitive miser is not only something we do, it's something we know our friends do as well. That's why Bethany's parents liked Hasan, but didn't want to spend the rest of their lives explaining prom pictures to friends and relatives. It's why befriending Scott felt like too big a risk for me to take. The Reeds liked the Hasan they knew. They also knew their friends wouldn't bother to know Hasan at all. Abiding by the boundary markers keeps us on the inside and others on the outside.

Being on the inside seems pretty important to us. Whether that means making it to the top, being respected by the guild, having adoring fans, being listened to by our peers, or being a household name. Being on the inside means we've made it and have been attested to by the group we believe is most important. We will reject one another, step over each other, and destroy others when their Otherness threatens our In-ness. We erect and nurture boundary markers because they give order to our lives and help us make sense of our world. But as easy as boundary markers are to maintain, we often miss the harmful effects of boundaries on nurturing beloved community. It's instinctive to create boundaries and feel threatened, so sometimes God has to be more direct, as God is with Peter: "The voice said to him again, a second time, 'What God has made clean, you must not call profane'" (Acts 10:15).

At first blush, this seems an odd place for God to make a point. What difference does Peter's diet make? Everyone has food they'd rather not eat. Many of my vegan friends find eating meat reprehensible but it's rarely a question of fellowship. You eat what you eat, and I'll eat what I eat. But, for Peter, the food is more than food. The unclean food represents unclean people. And even though Peter walked with Jesus, saw him heal a Centurion's daughter, dignify the Samaritan woman, make Samaritans heroes of parables, and heard him remind the Pharisees of the story of Naaman and the widow of Zeraphath, like many of us, what's known in the head is not alive in the heart. God had to arrange the circumstances for Peter to believe what he already knew. As the story unfolds, Cornelius's servants arrive, spend the night, and head back to Cornelius's home the next day. Luke captures Peter and Cornelius's bizarre introduction:

> The next day he got up and went with them, and some of the be-lievers from Joppa accompanied him. The following day they came to Caesarea. Cornelius was expecting them and had called togeth-er his relatives and close friends. On Peter's arrival Cornelius met him, and falling at his feet, worshiped him. But Peter made him get up, saying, "Stand up; I am only a mortal." And as he talked with him, he went in and found that many had assembled; and he said to them, "You yourselves know that it is unlawful for a Jew to associate with or to visit a Gentile; but God has shown me that I should not call anyone profane or unclean. So when I was sent for, I came without objection." (Acts 10:23b–28)

Peter's dream finally makes sense. Where he pushed backed against the dream, meeting Cornelius and Cornelius's family and friends in the flesh changed Peter's understanding of God's inclusion. This is what frequently happens when people are no longer abstractions. Our negative perceptions of others are almost always rooted in ignorance, difference, and indiffer-ence. As Martin Luther King Jr. said, "People fail to get along because they fear each other; they fear each other because they don't know each other; they don't know each other because they have not communicated with each other."[1] Peter, worshipping and serving his local and regional deity (YHWH), has to be broken out of a spiritual framework that understood God as merely local and regional. Peter's transformation takes both an en-counter with God and an encounter with Cornelius. New understandings of people and the embrace of Others is never simply an intellectual or aca-demic exercise. We can't actually know what God is doing without knowing the people God is doing it through. That's why it's dangerous for Christians to speak negatively about populations, whether they be racial, economic, religious, or national, whom they don't know. Even Peter, who walked with Jesus, lacked the depth of insight necessary to rightly discern what God was doing among people he didn't know. It takes contact to have impact! Anything less than real life contact creates caricatures of the Other; and caricatures lead to cruelty. It's simply too easy to talk about "those people,"

1. King, "Advice for Living."

74

when Others are distant, amorphous, and unknown. In the absence of first-hand knowledge, Others can easily become inhuman.

This simple meeting between Peter and Cornelius is enough to reshape Peter's imagination. In Peter's dream, when he first sees the blanket floating down from heaven, his initial response was litigation and argument. When that vision is made real in the flesh-and-blood person of Cornelius, the entire equation changes. Peter now remembers the Jesus who met the woman at the well and embraced outsiders and begins to do what he had seen Jesus do: teach in love. What first emerges from Peter's lips are words he might never have envisioned saying, "Then Peter began to speak to them: 'I truly understand that God shows no partiality, but in every nation anyone who fears him and does what is right is acceptable to him. You know the message he sent to the people of Israel, preaching peace by Jesus Christ—he is Lord of all'" (Acts 10:34–36).

Peter pronounces a second Pentecost! There in Cornelius's living room, the Spirit falls again. Only this time Peter's sermon isn't launched at the convicted heart of his hearers as it was in Acts 2. This time, Peter takes aim at his own soul. "God shows no partiality [favorites]," and "Jesus Christ—he is Lord of all." Again we see this beautiful, embracing, all-encompassing "all" of the Scriptures. What Peter learned is that God's embrace is larger and wholly enveloping.

It is inescapable that the Other is the very one God sends us to love and never the one to be marginalized, overlooked, and mistreated. Otherness is not an opportunity to practice estrangement. It is the central location where God is calling us to reflect Christ. Think of it this way: Had Bethany Reed's parents been Christians, Hasan's presence in their lives could have been God's doorway to demonstrate God's radical hospitality.

The Solution to Otherness

Others have always played a key role in the fulfillment of God's community living as God's people. It might surprise many Christians to learn that after serving as slaves for hundreds of years under the dictates of a brutal and violent regime in Egypt, many Egyptians sojourned alongside the Hebrews into the desert. Having witnessed the mighty acts of God, Egyptians who wanted to serve YHWH left Egypt with the former slaves. The newly freed Hebrews foreshadow the problem the Jews and Gentiles faced at the beginning of the church: How are all of these people supposed to live together?

As a solution, God gives Israel these instructions: "Don't take advantage of any stranger who lives in your land. You must treat the outsider as one of your native-born people—as a full citizen—and you are to love him in the same way you love yourself; for remember, you were once strangers living in Egypt. I am the Eternal One, your God" (Lev 19:33–34)? Shocking as it may sound, the Old Testament tradition offers a wider acceptance of the Other than almost any contemporary nation or organization. There has simply never been a secret handshake or pledging process in order for God-fearing people to treat everyone everywhere as brothers and sisters. One of my former professors, David Jensen, captures it this way: "The Other, according to this scriptural theme, is the one to whom we are summoned to love. Those who are different or alien, particularly those who are vulnerable, are afforded a distinct privilege: they are not regarded as 'lesser' citizens, beyond the pale of redemption, but as neighbors who are worthy of love in themselves, by the sheer fact that they are."[2] Jensen highlights what Peter and other Israelites had forgotten. The privileging of the Other is a response to having been slaves in Egypt. The Hebrews having been enslaved in a brutal, racially and religiously based system are not to perpetuate that system by engineering their own. They are to move the other direction, to be more inclusive and embracing than any people in the history of the world. Here we see the institution of what later peoples will call the Golden Rule—"do unto others"—but when this theme first appears, the direction is outward toward those farthest outside our personal boundary marker. The Jews were not to return the distancing, estrangement, and Otherness they experienced. As the descendent of slaves in America, I cannot imagine the sense of injustice and the desire for revenge my great-grandparents would have felt had their captors suddenly reversed themselves and desired to join the community. Yet this is what the power and Spirit of God does and has always done. God's love meets disassociation with connection. This is the lesson of Peter and Cornelius and the lesson for the church.

We should not be naïve. Neither Peter nor contemporary Christians can bridge the gap between people by ascending shaky scaffolding. Even after Peter has this experience with Cornelius, the leftover racial and religious privilege he learned from childhood still erupted.

In those early days of the church, James, Peter, and Paul agreed that the best way to reach greater numbers of people with the message of Jesus was to form a two-headed snake. Though all three men were Jewish, since James

2. Jensen, *In The Company of Others*, 3.

and Peter were well respected among the Jews, they would focus their work and attention on teaching and ministering to the Jewish population. Paul would focus on ministry to the Gentiles (likely because many Jews remembered him as "Saul" and would be slow to trust him). This dual-pronged approach meant that James and Peter maintained all their Jewish traditions and customs, but Paul, like all good missionaries, did not have the luxury of playing on his home court. All the Jewish customs that formed barriers between Jews and Gentiles had not only been removed by Jesus's death, but because they no longer functioned, were abandoned by Paul in favor of behaviors that would be more effective at reaching his new community. Peter, when working alongside Paul in Gentile communities, is willing to lay aside his Jewish traditions—those markers that defined him as one of God's people—but loses his nerve when other Jews arrive. Some Jewish disciples of Jesus believed Gentile believers should convert to Judaism and subject themselves to Jewish practices as a prerequisite to accepting Jesus. When Paul sees Peter revert to practices that drew lines and refused to accept all that God had made as good, Paul drops to DEFCON 1.

> But when Cephas [Peter] came to Antioch, there was a problem. I got in his face and exposed him in front of everyone. He was clearly wrong. Here's what was going on: before certain people from James arrived, Cephas used to share meals with the Gentile outsiders. And then, after they showed up, Cephas suddenly became aloof and distanced himself from the outsiders because he was afraid of those believers who thought circumcision was necessary. (Gal 2:11–12)

Paul sees the inevitable dis-integration of the church if Otherness and disjunction are allowed to burrow themselves under the skin of the infant church. It cannot be allowed to gestate. If Peter severs the ties of fellowship over racial, religious, socioeconomic, or hierarchical matters, it becomes easier for others to follow suit and continue a destructive pattern of sequestration and isolation. Paul speaks to Peter in the strongest possible terms:

> The rest of the Jewish believers followed his lead, including Barnabas! Their hypocritical behavior was so obvious—their actions were not at all consistent with everything the good news of our Lord represents. So I approached Cephas and told him in plain sight of everyone: "If you, a Jew, have lived like the Gentile outsiders and not like the Jews, then how can you turn around and urge the outsiders to start living like Jews?" We are natural-born Jews, not sinners from the godless nations. But we know that no one is made right with God by meeting the demands of the law. It is

only through the faithfulness of Jesus the Anointed that salvation is even possible. This is why we put faith in Jesus the Anointed: so we will be put right with God. It's His faithfulness—not works prescribed by the law—that puts us in right standing with God because no one will be acquitted and declared "right" for doing what the law demands. (Gal 2:13–16 The Voice).

Innuendo is not one of Paul's strengths. Peter is scolded with little tenderness. Peter had forgotten Pentecost. Peter had forgotten an afternoon at Cornelius's house. Look how far Peter has fallen. When Peter meets Cornelius's family and friends, full of the Holy Spirit, he proclaims, "It is clear to me now that God plays no favorites, that God accepts every person whatever his or her culture or ethnic background, that God welcomes all who revere Him and do right" (Acts 10:34 The Voice). Peter reverted to the rootless, fruitless vestiges of a pre-Jesus religion. And that's what religious expressions that nurture divisions are, rootless and fruitless. Paul unloads a double-barreled assault on Peter's behaviors. And he should have.

My heart aches for Hasan Minhaj, whiling away the night, dressed for prom, playing *Mario Kart*. He can't share his sorrow with his family. His friends are dancing the night away. I bet his classmates peppered a red-faced Bethany, "Where's Hasan?" Hasan is completely alone in the world.

That's what Otherness does to people. It abandons them.

Mrs. Reed isn't some lone malicious woman in the world, though we'd like to make her out to be one. The truth is, Mrs. Reed stole her lines from one of the first Christians and an apostle of the church: "We think you're great, we really love having you over, but . . . we're going to be taking a lot of pictures tonight . . . and, um, we just don't think it'd be a good fit. Do you need a ride home?"

There is a simple truth that twenty-first-century Christians can no longer avoid: When we distance ourselves from the Other, whether it be based on race, religion, gender, sexuality, lifestyle, economics, politics, or any number of cherished divisions, we might as well say, "It's time for you to go home."

8

Choosing Sides

I don't really understand it. Never have. The more I think
on it the more it horrifies me. How can they look in the eyes
of a man and make a slave of him and then quote the Bible?

—Michael Shaara, *The Killer Angels*

MEDGAR EVERS WAS SHOT and killed while unloading a box of T-shirts
from the trunk of his car. The shirts read, "Jim Crow Must Go." A
bullet from an M1917 Enfield rifle ripped through the heart of the young
civil rights activist in Jackson, Mississippi, on June 12, 1963. Medgar Evers
was a World War II veteran and college graduate, but that meant very little
in Mississippi in the 1960s. After leaving the army, Evers put his education
and skills to work for the cause of equality. The night he was assassinated,
Evers, then field secretary for the NAACP, had attended an organizational
meeting in the wake of President John Kennedy's Civil Rights Address,
which had been delivered earlier that evening. The combustible mixture
of hand-me-down racism, fears of a changing culture, and the burgeoning
influence of the civil rights movement inevitably led to murderous action.
Medgar Evers was one of the untold hundreds who paid the full cost of
equality with his own blood and death.

After the bullet entered his back, Evers stumbled several feet before
collapsing. He was rushed to a local Jackson hospital where he was denied
admittance because of his color. Only after learning who he was did the
hospital relent and offer care. It was too late. Fifty minutes after he was shot,
Medgar Evers died.

Medgar Evers was murdered in his driveway.

My father knew that driveway.

My father was Medgar Evers's paperboy.

Dr. Richard Palmer Sr., my dad, was finishing the seventh grade when Byron De La Beckwith, a member of the White Citizens' Council, later called the Ku Klux Klan, shot Evers. Every day after school my dad would load up his books, walk a mile in the opposite direction of his own house because, "The Evers lived over there in Shady Acres, where the middle-class blacks lived," and worked his daily paper route. Dad witnessed the hateful world of segregation and division that led to violence up close.

The marks of fragile white supremacy had expressed itself in violence at the Evers' home before. A month before Evers's assassination my dad threw the Evers' paper, and all was normal. The next day there was burned wood and singed bricks—the aftermath of a Molotov cocktail. Distressed racists repeatedly attempted to threaten and intimidate Evers in their pitifully faithless attempts to hold on to their imperiled, but godless, illusions of superiority. A month after the Molotov cocktail, Medgar Evers was murdered.

When I was a boy in Mississippi, things weren't that different than when my father grew up in Mississippi. It was a world whose vision mostly came in black and white. It was a divided world. And the truth is, the world has not changed much. Our public language may have changed, but the defects of the human heart have not.

In the spring of 2014 a group of fraternity brothers from Sigma Alpha Epsilon from The University of Oklahoma were videoed chanting that "niggers" would never be accepted in their fraternity. The boys stood in their charter bus, fueled by alcohol and ignorance, chanting, "There will never be a nigger SAE. You can hang him from a tree, but he can never sign with me. There will never be a nigger SAE." We like to think that the world, that America, is different than it was in 1963, but apparently it is not. Millennial college students have not been inoculated from the vitiating virus of divisions, factions, and racism. There is a malformation in the human soul that nurtures divisions and enjoys picking sides. Left unchecked, this malformation leads to cancers such as Byron De La Beckwith. It's left to Christians to push against these forces. To ignore the power of division and derision, as some churches have, or to passively accept such divisions, abandons the gospel of which Paul is not ashamed.

Jersey Sunday

At The Vine Church, where I pastored for five years, one of our great annual traditions was "Jersey Sunday." On the first Sunday of the NFL season we invited everyone to come to worship donning their jerseys from their favorite sports team. I live in Texas. Texas is football country. From high school to college to the NFL, fall is for football. Except at The Vine, we celebrated two kinds of football, and on Jersey Sunday we have more fútbol jerseys than all other sports combined. We were largely a soccer church, but if you want to start a fight, talk American football. On Jersey Sunday, there's no shortage of Dallas Cowboys and Houston Texans jerseys, but they don't compare to the abundance of Texas Longhorns, Texas A&M, and even Texas Tech Red Raiders apparel. The congregation is one hour from the University of Texas at Austin and an hour and a half from Texas A&M. The congregation is a divided house, and if we weren't all Christians there might be blood on the pulpit. In Texas football is felt and experienced deeply. But we're not alone. Americans love sports and their sports teams. Football, more than anything, is our game.

In 2016 at the Republican National Convention, Speaker of the House Paul Ryan addressed the Texas delegation about party unity. A year earlier, presidential candidate and Texas Senator Ted Cruz was running for the Republican Presidential nomination against eventual nominee, Donald Trump. While Trump won the nomination, Cruz won Texas, and Ryan was doing his dead-level best to get the Texas delegation to throw their support behind Trump. In doing so, Ryan proved he was not from Texas. As the Speaker was trying to rouse support for a united front, he deployed the metaphor of football, saying, "You've got Horned Frogs, Aggies . . . You've got Longhorns . . . But when one of the teams advances, to a big bowl game? Or a national championship? Don't you root for the Aggies if you are a Longhorn?" The crowd broke out in laughter—and boos, by some reports. "You don't? . . . Well, let me tell you how we do it where I come from." Nothing reveals the depths of our allegiances like sports. So when we talk about how we ought to talk to and the way we treat one another, our emotional investment in sports might be instructive.

In Christena Cleveland's book *Disunity in Christ*, the sociologist recounts the story of a football game between Dartmouth and Princeton in 1951. It's not quite Texas vs. Texas A&M, but a rivalry is a rivalry. The game was unbelievably brutal. By the end of the third quarter, a Dartmouth player's leg had been broken and a Princeton player's nose was broken—and this was before athletes were as big and fast as they are now. Both teams received multiple penalties. In the aftermath, researchers at Dartmouth and Princeton took the game as an opportunity to conduct an experiment. They wanted to measure the fans' perceptions of why the game was so rough. The researchers discovered that both groups believed that their teams were less responsible for the foul play than the rival team. "It was their fault. They're the problem." Even though both teams were heavily penalized, neither side was willing to admit their team contributed to the problem—at least not nearly as much as the other team. Add to that recent surveys dealing with Social Identification Theory and sports. People feel better and have greater self-esteem when their team wins. Sports have the ability to increase our self-esteem by affiliation and association. When we wear jerseys or buy tickets to the game or follow the stats, we feel that we are somehow integral to the success or failure of the team.

The team is *us*. We are the team. When the team wins, we feel like winners along with them. But the rabbit hole goes even deeper. In England, where fútbol (soccer) is the most followed sport, team affiliation often has both racial and economic roots. Soccer fans sing during matches and teams' racial and economic roots are often recounted through club traditions and songs. It's embedded in the identity of the team.

The English Premier League club Tottenham Hotspurs is located in north London. The club was extremely popular with Jewish immigrants to the United Kingdom during the nineteenth and twentieth centuries. Many Jews settled near the club and to this day supporters (fans) refer to themselves as the "Yid Army." Though "Yid" is technically a racial slur, Spurs supporters have owned it. Likewise, other European soccer clubs, like Ajax in Amsterdam, have had a long history of Jewish support. Because the clubs have Jewish histories, opposing fans jeer both the athletes and their fans using racially charged slurs. In the 1980s when reports of soccer hooliganism were widespread, American sports fans, as fanatical as they are, did not understand people coming to blows during soccer games. What they didn't know was the racial and economic enmity that fueled the divisions coupled with the human propensity to choose sides and defend them.

These stories are merely fascinating events until social identification theory flows into "it's the other team's fault," and crests over the banks until it spills into ethnic and racial tension, segregation, and violence. We had Jersey Sunday at The Vine each year to remind ourselves of one simple fact:

one of the easier things to do is choose sides. When we choose sides, those on the other side become opponents to be defeated.

One of the impulses that causes side choosing against others, rather than for others, is our own deeply felt need for self-esteem. Part of what gives us our self-esteem are the sides we choose and the groups we belong to. This easy choosing of sides is a key hurdle to living in beloved community.

What people do is pick a group to belong to and then perceive life through the lens of whether or not some event makes our group look good or bad. Like our sports teams, when our group looks good we feel better about ourselves. We then amplify what makes us look good and minimize what makes us look bad. Once sides are chosen, life becomes an infinite loop of image management and excuse making to reinforce the rattletrap structures of our frail psyches. Social psychologist Jonathan Haidt captures it this way: "when people all share values, when people all share morals, they become a team, and once you engage the psychology of teams, it shuts down open-minded thinking."

Not convinced? Maybe a story will help. In Luke, Jesus launches a story about the dangers of choosing sides: "He [Jesus] told another parable—this one addressed to people who were confident in their self-righteousness and looked down on other people with disgust" (Luke 18:9 The Voice). Jesus is encountering people who have a high view of themselves, but a low view of others. Do you know people like this? Do you ever see it in politics? Do you know someone who has strong political opinions and the people on the other side of the aisle can never be right about anything, ever? This is what choosing sides does. Someone is a Democrat? Must have a mental disorder and be morally bankrupt. On the other side, someone is a Republican? Must be fundamentally flawed and greedy. The other side never has a point. Only my side of the aisle is righteous. We're always right. When we do admit we're wrong, there's always a mitigating circumstance or some moral equivalency that makes our shortcomings anomalous or understandable. When we're wrong the other side is more wrong.

Have you ever known anyone whose theology or church practices could never be wrong? They couldn't possibly be mistaken. When I was a boy, we called people in other churches "the denominations." This was our passive-aggressive way of being self-righteous and looking down on others with disgust. As Jesus reveals, it was a lesson we should have learned from our equally self-righteous ancestors.

> Jesus: Imagine two men *walking up a road*, going to the temple
> to pray. One of them is a Pharisee and the other is a *despised* tax
> collector. Once inside the temple, the Pharisee stands up and prays
> this prayer in honor of himself: "God, how I thank You that I am
> not on the same level as other people—crooks, cheaters, the sexu-
> ally immoral—like this tax collector over here. *Just look at me!* I
> fast *not once but* twice a week, and I faithfully pay my tithes on
> every penny of income." Over in the corner, the tax collector be-
> gins to pray, but he won't even lift his eyes to heaven. He pounds
> on his chest *in sorrow* and says, "God, be merciful to me, a sinner!"
>   *Now imagine these two men walking back down the road to
> their homes.* Listen, it's the tax collector who walks home clean
> before God, and not the Pharisee, because whoever lifts himself up
> will be put down and whoever takes a humble place will be lifted
> up. (Luke 18:10–14 The Voice)

The most obvious aspect of this story is the self-righteousness of the
Pharisee and the humility of the tax collector. What is more curious is the
screwball oddness of the Pharisee's prayer. It would never occur to most
people to inaugurate a prayer by telling God how awesome we are. "You
know God, you might have missed this. I didn't get a card or anything. I
didn't see a bonus check, but I'm doing a pretty bang-up job down here.
You might want to spread the word, God, because I'm knocking it out of
the ballpark." None of us would pray that. And my guess is that no Pharisee
would either. Pharisees were particular about the language they used when
talking to God. No Pharisee would dare say this, just like none of us would
say it . . . *out loud*! Though we might not say this audibly, we might say it to
ourselves. We all face the temptation of perceiving the world on the basis
of what makes us and our group look good or what serves our agenda. We
might say something that upholds the goodness of our team while we look
down on others. We've chosen sides. We spend a great deal of our lives
vindicating the sides we've chosen. In the Pharisees' mind, he's on the right
side. He's a member of the right group. The other guy is a tax collector, a
Roman collaborator. Wrong group. Unequivocally wrong. Always wrong.

Rage Against the Machines

Jesus's story is deceptive because it sounds like Jesus is talking about an
interpersonal conflict. It's just one guy thinking he's better than the other
guy. That's too simplistic. Jesus is telling a social story. It's a story about two

groups. It's a story about systems. If Jesus had wanted to tell an interpersonal story he would have. He would have said, "two men went to the temple," just like he said, "a certain man owned a vineyard," or "a man had two sons." Jesus knows how to tell that kind of story. Rather, Jesus wants you to know that one man identifies as part of a group, a Pharisee! The other man is part of another group, Roman collaborators. The groups they belong to affect how the Pharisee sees himself and how he sees the tax collector. Pharisees are winners and tax collectors are losers. The hierarchy is set. The Pharisee knows where things align on the totem pole. When we become defined by which side we've chosen, we become both defensive and aggressive toward other groups. The word for that is "combative." The fault belongs with the other guy and we feel better when our team wins.

The Pharisee Jesus speaks of doesn't know this tax collector. He doesn't know his heart nor his story. He doesn't know if he has a wife and kids or what stressors he's facing. This Pharisee doesn't know why the tax collector became a tax collector. He only knows he *is* a tax collector and that's all he thinks needs to know. Perhaps there is someone in your life who you've defined by group (Black, white, Mexican, immigrant, Democrat, Republican, Muslim, Gay, Straight). You don't know them, their desires, stories, hurts, or dreams, but because they belong to a different group, you think you know all you need to know. Social-Identification prevents us from seeing and hearing one another. If someone criticizes our group's theology or lifestyle or political ideology, we are unable to receive it because we are too busy protecting our group identity, wearing our jersey. Sadly, many within the Christian community not only tolerate the choosing of sides, they actively promote it as a means of church growth and peace.

The Same Kind of Same as Me

While Jesus highlights the self-aggrandizing threats of choosing sides, in the late twentieth and early twenty-first century, the Christian community in America transmitted the social virus to new church plants through a precept commonly called the Homogeneous Unit Principle (HUP).[1] An easy way to

1. Some readers will know the Homogeneous Unit Principle as a sociological principle regarding how people make choices, having little to do with ecclesiology. This is true in a broad sense. Here, I'm interested in how churches have embraced and deployed this principle to grow churches in terms of numerical increase to the detriment of discipleship.

understand the principle is that it's easier for non-believers to discover Christ when there are fewer barriers to cross. On its face it makes sense. Coming to Christ requires crossing a large threshold from disbelief to belief. To lessen the disorientation, the Homogeneous Unit Principle recommends removing racial, class, economic, and educational impediments in order to help Christians reach more people for Christ. By "removing" they mean focusing their energies on particular demographics and structuring communal life around the preferences and experiences of those demographics. One big barrier is enough, they suggest. In the most generous light the Homogenous Unit Principle places the person of Jesus at the center of the conversion experience, but it is undoubtedly shortsighted. In some sections of the Christian community, conversion is a shallow pool. It's a conversation designed to calcify what's already wrong in the human heart. The Homogeneous Unit Principle wins people to Jesus in the sense that they've moved from one set of mental and behavioral commitments to another, but only a few commitments. It loses people in that from the start they are taught that death to self is an adjunct to the Christian life. The Homogenous Unit Principle works well to build crowds and make church-goers; it doesn't begin to touch discipleship. It cannot touch discipleship because it overlooks the central issue of the earliest church. While we can acknowledge the purity of heart within the architects of the Homogenous Unit Principle, we would be ill-served to discount the ways they have unmoored the church from the gospel proclaimed by Jesus and Paul. We cannot behave as if Jesus's prayer, "May they be one even as We are one" (John 17:11), was never prayed. This affection for homogeneity has produced what theologian Scot McKnight calls, "a fellowship of sames." In essence, we gather with others who look, sound, think, and behave like us, allowing us to maintain racial, religious, and economic distance, as well as the ignorance and prejudice that often resides in cultural illiteracy.

As we discussed earlier, the blood pumping within Paul's letter to the Romans, as well as the navigating principle underlying Peter's encounter with Cornelius, was the coming together of all people under the banner of Christ. Paul makes this clear in 2 Corinthians 5:15–16: "He died for us so that we will all live, not for ourselves, but for Him who died and rose from the dead. Because of all that God has done, we now have a new perspective. We used to show regard for people based on worldly standards and interests. No longer. We used to think of the Anointed the same way. No longer." Where Paul calls us to a "new perspective," the Homogenous Unit Principle accepts and ordains our immersion in our old perspectives. Instead of being called-out of our false-selves and ego, homogeneity baptizes those egos and lifts them to the level of strategic thinking. The Homogeneous Unit Principle would have us leap over the imperatives of the gospel in order to make church membership easier. We can build bigger barns and call them churches. In essence, communities rooted in the Homogenous Unit Principle have little heartburn allowing congregants to maintain their racial, religious, and economic sides. And though we deny it, the church's silence about choosing sides creates the murderous imaginations of men like Byron De La Beckwith, and American history is its own proof.

Homogeneity and Hostility

If you grew up in America, you know about Harriet Beecher Stowe's *Uncle Tom's Cabin*. Stowe's *Uncle Tom's Cabin* is a fictional tale about the horrors of slavery in the United States. In the nineteenth century *Uncle Tom's Cabin* was second in sales only to the Bible, and it is largely credited with aiding the burgeoning abolitionist movement to end slavery.

A less well-known novel is E. W. Warren's *Nellie Norton, or, Southern Slavery and the Bible: A Scriptural Refutation of the Principal Arguments upon which the Abolitionists Rely. A Vindication of Southern Slavery from the Old and New Testaments.* It's a fictional story too.

In November 1859 Nellie Norton, a beautiful young New England woman, believes slavery is immoral and cruel. Nellie travels with her mother to Savannah, Georgia, to visit relatives who own a plantation worked by slaves. After arguing with family members, Nellie determines she is wrong about slavery. Nellie discovers that slave owners are victims of "malignant abuse" and "wicked and malicious slander" by ignorant, ar- rogant Northerners; the world is wrong and the South must set it right; that the world is in error and is dependent upon the South for the truth. Nellie concludes that the welfare of the negro is best promoted when he is under the restraints of slavery, and that slavery is the normal condition of the negro. As the novel ends, Nellie falls in love with a handsome and charming slave owner. Nellie and her new husband turn their home into a hospital for wounded confederate soldiers.

E. W. Warren was a southern preacher. He read his Bible, prayed to God, and preached sermons. Every fiber in Warren's body believed in Jesus. I'm sure he tried his best to follow Jesus. He was simply ignorant of the myriad ways an enchantment with sameness increasingly leads to discrimination. Exclusion never starts with exclusion. It begins with distance. Distance leads to ignorance. Ignorance leads to fear. Fear leads to violence. And some churches are deliberately starting the countdown sequence to prejudice in the misguided effort to be large at all cost. We have forgotten that what we win people with is what we win people to. Though the Homogenous Unit Principle is not solely to blame, one reason Sunday morning remains the most segregated time of the week is that church leaders have chosen for it to be so. There is simply no way to read Paul in his context seriously and find adherence to this principle acceptable.

The gospel, as preached by Jesus and Paul, is the antidote to, not the safe house of, homogeneity. The point is to bring those we consider Other together in loving, healing, and reconciling ways. This is why Paul announces in Galatians,

> But now that true faith has come, we have no need for a tutor. It is your faith in the Anointed Jesus that makes all of you children of God because all of you who have been initiated into the Anointed One through the ceremonial washing of baptism have put Him on. It makes no difference whether you are a Jew or a Greek, a slave or a freeman, a man or a woman, because in Jesus the Anointed, the Liberating King, you are all one. Since you belong to Him and are now subject to His power, you are the descendant of Abraham and the heir of God's glory according to the promise. (Gal 3:25–29 The Voice)

Oneness is not incidental to the purpose of the gospel. Yet a church riveted to the Homogenous Church Principle must make integration an adjunct (read: optional) pursuit to the gospel, in order to justify its own evangelistic strategy. The bridging of Jew and Greek, slave and free, man and woman must be relegated to secondary status or somehow pinned-in to local and particular concerns in Galatia, but Paul has a cosmic and universal perspective. The death of Jesus, which vindicated him as the true God, eliminates the differences between people that don't make a difference. What's more, Paul roots this new creation in the person of Abraham, the Hebrew who does not receive his Judaism through birth or the works of Torah, but through faith. Byron De La Beckwith, E. W. Warren, and countless others believe in God, but they believe in a particularly narrow God because their churches never told them not to. The results of that belief are exposed in hatred and violence. It always has. Homogeneity allows us to institutionalize our side choosing.

One might think that too much is being made of all this and segregated churches couldn't possibly lead to hostility and murder. It would be easy to believe too much is being made of this except that the Apostle Paul explained this path centuries ago. Writing to the church in Ephesus, Paul encourages the church:

> He is the embodiment of our peace, sent once and for all to take down the great barrier of hatred and hostility that has divided us so that we can be one. He offered His body on the sacrificial altar to bring an end to the law's ordinances and dictations that separated Jews from the outside nations. His desire was to create in His body one new humanity from the two opposing groups, thus creating peace. Effectively the cross becomes God's means to kill off the hostility once and for all so that He is able to reconcile them both to God in this one new body. (Eph 2:14–16 The Voice)

Jesus's cross ends hostility by forming one group out of two. Hostility is more than simple discomfort. It is greater than misunderstanding or disregard. Hostility is antagonism fortified by aggression. When wars are ended, we call it "a ceasing of hostilities." Yet the Homogeneous Unit Principle allows Christians to nurture enmity under the withering fig leaf of church growth. Astute Christians are beginning to ask whether churches warmed in the incubator of homogeneity are actually churches at all.

Christians must abandon the denuded, silicon-filled mannequin we have nourished through homogeneity and seek a more robust, vibrant, and real expression of one body. The old creation is gone. To hold on to her decaying form is like lying next to a dead body and hoping it will bring you life. It will draw a crowd, but it will not transform the crowd for the better. The gospel shows us how to deal with racial, economic, and educational barriers: the Homogeneous Unit Principle teaches us not to bother at all. The church must embrace an alternative approach to the world that learns to choose differently.

One of the least understood stories in the life of Jesus is that of the Rich Young Ruler. In Matthew 19, Jesus has been teaching and there are a string of people approaching him, asking questions, seeking healing, or just wanting to be near Jesus.

> Just then a man came up to Jesus and asked, "Teacher, what good thing must I do to get eternal life?"
> "Why do you ask me about what is good?" Jesus replied. "There is only One who is good. If you want to enter life, keep the commandments."
> "Which ones?" he inquired.

Jesus replied, "'You shall not murder, you shall not commit adultery, you shall not steal, you shall not give false testimony, honor your father and mother,' and 'love your neighbor as yourself.'"

"All these I have kept," the young man said. "What do I still lack?"

Jesus answered, "If you want to be perfect, go, sell your possessions and give to the poor, and you will have treasure in heaven. Then come, follow me."

When the young man heard this, he went away sad, because he had great wealth. Then Jesus said to his disciples, "Truly I tell you, it is hard for someone who is rich to enter the kingdom of heaven. Again I tell you, it is easier for a camel to go through the eye of a needle than for someone who is rich to enter the kingdom of God." (Matt 19:16–24 NRSV)

"What good thing must I do to get eternal life?" is a great question and the very question those practicing the Homogeneous Unit Principle are trying to make easier for seekers. But this young man has a problem. He has a lot of money and the status and privileges that comes with wealth. Like the Pharisee, he knows where he sits on the totem pole, yet he desires the right things. Matthew never suggests the man has a bad heart or is trying to trick Jesus. He's sincere. Jesus thinks he's sincere, too. The instructions are simple: "Go sell all of your stuff and give it to the poor. Then you'll have treasure in heaven." The young man doesn't like Jesus's response. You and I don't like it either. In fact, this story should scare every one of us. By worldly standards the majority of American Christians are the rich, young ruler. We have all we need and more. Our anxiety gets stirred, not when we fear we lack our daily bread, but over fears of lacking bread thirty or forty years in the future. "Daily" has become decades. Jesus has us in his sight. So, when Jesus comes along saying to inherit eternal life we must sell our possessions and give the proceeds to the poor, we want to find the escape clause. It's just not there. Jesus either has to be talking to just this one guy—it was just a message for him—or we're just going to ignore Jesus on this one.

Nowhere in Scripture is it suggested that Jesus was talking only to the rich, young ruler. Matthew doesn't write in the margin, "Oh, by the way, Jesus met this one guy and had a word just for him and no one else." Plus, we don't treat other teachings of Jesus as if he were only talking to one person. We don't say that about "take up your cross and follow me," or "surely I will be with you always." When Jesus speaks, we assume He's talking to all of us.

At the same time, after Jesus ascends to the right hand of the Father, nowhere in the Scriptures do we hear the apostles instructing the fledgling church to sell everything and give it to the poor. Though generosity was always central and while many disciples sold a great deal of their possessions to support the young church, selling everything and giving it to the poor is never commanded nor instructed as normative. Many of the apostles, like Jesus their Master, chose homelessness and moved from house to house, but we never hear the apostles complaining, "I don't know what's wrong with these people. We can't get them to sell all their possessions and give it to the poor. They must not be serious Christians." The apostles didn't interpret Jesus's interaction with the rich young ruler as only pertaining to him, nor did they see it pertaining to everyone for all time. There is something more beautiful and profound happening here that has little to do with riches or young and has everything to do with solidarity. Jesus's deeper point is one that is passed on to future disciples. To be perfect, Jesus explains, the rich, young ruler needs to embrace the experiences of the Other. Disciples are instructed to choose the Other's side. When a rich, young ruler sells his possessions and gives to the poor, he gets to experience life as the poor experience life. The rich, young ruler gets to *be* poor. He doesn't merely get to sympathize with the poor. He has to join them. To inherit eternal life means aligning yourself with those on the other side; seeing life through their eyes; acquiring their experiences as your own. Modern churches tell America's rich, young rulers to find other rich, young rulers to worship alongside. You can come to Jesus and keep your social and cultural barriers just where they are, because we don't intend to challenge them. Jesus shows us that while we've been busy picking, choosing, and protecting our sides, eternal life is found in choosing the other side, playing for the other team.

In the fall of 2015, Kim Davis was arrested for failing to comply with a judge's order to issue marriage licenses to same-sex couples. Mrs. Davis, the Rowan County, Kentucky, clerk, had burned up headlines and news feeds because of her unwillingness to follow the Supreme Court's *Obergefell v. Hodges* ruling making gay marriage legal in all fifty states. In her opposition the *Obergefell* ruling, Davis also rejected a court order. For Mrs. Davis, gay marriage is against God's will and she believes it would be a violation of her religious beliefs to aid those unions. That's a fair argument to make. Historically, Muslims, Jews, and Christians, have considered same-sex relationships out of step with God's will. Even as mores concerning marriage fluctuate in American culture, many, if not most, Christians oppose gay-marriage for religious reasons. When asked about her refusal to follow the law, Mrs. Davis, responded, "It is not a light issue for me. It is a Heaven or Hell decision." This is clearly a response of personal conscience for her and many others, but how could this understanding of Jesus's interaction with the rich, young ruler reshape her response? In short, Kim Davis believes that participating in what she considers a sinful act—though it's not her marriage and she has likely signed marriage licenses for adulterous couples and couples that have engaged in fornication and premartial sex—puts her at risk of eternal damnation. But if she, along with Christian photographers and bakers who are disquieted by the increasing demands to provide services for gay weddings, were equally devoted to the story of the rich, young ruler, they would understand that the loving, God-like position is to choose solidarity with the Other. When we understand the Other, not as one to be opposed, and definitely not as one to be oppressed, but as one to be joined, our engagement with the world fundamentally shifts. Instead of stone-faced, domineering contention, the church would choose comradeship and simple kindness. Not only might Christian county clerks, photographers, and bakers serve those whose lifestyles they find demeritorious, they would serve them gladly. What if when faced with these challenges, Christian businesspersons and civic officers went out of their way to understand and serve the Other? What if those of us following Jesus's example of incarnational living asked same-sex couples how they met and endeavored to understand their stories. What if we provided services free of charge, performing our duties kindly and with excellence, and keeping a door open for relationship building? As Kim Davis refused service to same-sex couples in Kentucky, the nightly news footage showed images of couples shouting at her. Absolutely no one left those interactions closer to God. It is the kind of exchange that serves cable news, politicians, and the forces of evil well, but leaves all those engaged farther from Jesus.

The Prison Nun

In 2013, I read the obituary of a nun I'd never heard about. Antonia Brenner, better known as Mother Antonia, is also called "The Prison Nun." Mother Antonia was born Mary Brenner Clark and lived a privileged life in Beverly Hills. She was a blonde, southern California socialite. As the twice-divorced mother of seven, Mother Antonia was banned from joining any existing religious order. She started one of her own. Mother Antonia was deeply rooted in a vision of God that lead her to solidarity with the poor, broken, wounded, and distressed. While she could have done anything, Mother Antonia chose ministry at the maximum-security La Mesa Prison in Tijuana, Mexico. La Mesa is one of the most dangerous prisons in the world filled with Mexico's most notorious and violent criminals. These men have murdered, raped, and beaten people in their lives, but when Mother Antonia comes around they melt. They are known to reach through the bars shouting for her to please come visit them today. To the guards and warden, the prisoners are some of the most violent and dangerous men alive. When Mother Antonia comes around the prisoners turn into family. Mother Antonia was neither a prisoner nor a guard, but she became the connection between the two groups. The warden and the prisoners, each hardened by and opposed to each other in myriad ways, came to trust her as someone of goodwill, fairness, and reconciliation.

A few years before her death, Mother Antonia was visiting her family in Beverly Hills. While she was away a prison riot broke out. Some of the inmates killed guards and took their weapons. The riot became so violent the warden evacuated the remaining guards and shut off the power to the prison. When Mother Antonia got news of the riot, she came back immediately and asked to be allowed in the prison to talk to "her boys." The warden refused. He told her of the danger of going in, and how the Mexican federales had surrounded the entire prison and were about to assault the facility.

But Mother Antonia knew something that the warden didn't. Love never fails. Solidarity is a means of salvation. These were "her boys."

Eventually she wore down the warden and he allowed her to enter the prison. The prison was totally dark. Mother Antonia pleaded with the inmates to put down their guns before anyone else got hurt. After a few minutes they came out and one inmate told her, "As soon as we heard your voice we threw our guns out the window, Mother."

Mother Antonia was no trained negotiator. The reason she brought peace out of hostility is that every day, after she finished praying with the inmates and taking their confessions, when she was done with her counseling and teaching, she didn't go home to her nice, comfortable suburban house in Tijuana. Instead, Mother Antonia walked down the hallway and laid her head down in the eight-by-ten cell that she lived in for thirty years. Mother Antonia began working at La Mesa in 1977. As different as they are from her, she chose to experience what her boys experienced. She chose their side.

9

War and Peace

It is the Holy Spirit's job to convict, God's job to judge, and
my job to love.

—Billy Graham

W HEN I ENTERED MINISTRY, the first big, all-church event I hosted was
a marriage seminar. I found a couple I really liked from California,
Dennis and Emily Lowe, to serve as facilitators for the weekend. Rochelle
and I had met them briefly six months earlier at a marriage and family conference and were moved by their story. When we first met the Lowes they'd
been married to each other for nearly twenty-five years. Both were licensed
therapists and had two young sons. They were just what I was looking for.

The Saturday of the seminar, the Lowes walked our group—about
thirty couples—through strategies of communicating during difficult
times. In essence, they told us how to have a productive disagreement with
your spouse.

The method was reflective listening. After your spouse said something, you were supposed to reply, "What I hear you saying is . . . " and
repeat their comment back to them. The entire system is designed to de-
escalate highly volatile and emotionally tinged issues that arise in marriage.
Once you master it, reflective listening works wonderfully well.

As our couples were learning to communicate without animosity and
attack, one of our church members raised her hand. She said, "I don't think
this'll ever work in my marriage."

"Why not?" the facilitator asked.

"Well, I don't know about anybody else here—this seems nice and all—but when I fight, I wanna have a fight."

For some of us, there is something satisfying about fighting. Maybe it's the emotional release. Maybe some of us didn't get the pony we wanted when we were kids and we enter conflict already resenting our position in life. Maybe there's something about throwing punches that makes us feel strong. Fighting makes a us feel alive and vigorous. At its best, fighting can remind us that we care about meaningful and important issues. Anger isn't always bad. But sometimes, we just like to fight.

Win at All Cost?

The Roman Empire liked to fight, too. When it came to armed empires, the Romans were like no other. Only they tried to convince the world that their fighting was designed to create peace—a notion governments, even now, try to pass off as genuine. You may have heard about the Roman approach; it was called the *Pax Romana*, the peace of Rome. It was peace at the end of the sword, peace enforced by fear and blood and graves. Rome conquered nations, disarmed citizens, repressed ideas and dissent, and wielded an unforgiving blade. Few would stand up to Rome. Few would push back or advocate their rights. Rome brought peace, for sure—a gangland sort of peace.

You can imagine then that Christians in Rome, living in the freedom of Christ but under the foot of Rome, wanted to give Rome a taste of its own version of peace. Most of us, too, would be tempted to fight back. As a matter of fact, fighting back is the language we hear and use in our contemporary cultural battles as various sides jockey for cultural prominence.

American Christians displayed our willingness to fight fire with fire in 2012 when Dan Cathy, a professed Christian and Chief Operating Officer of Chick-Fil-A, made public his private thoughts about homosexuality and gay marriage. Unfortunately, those opposed to Cathy responded with their own threats and anger. As the wheel spun around, Christians across America staged a Chick-Fil-A Appreciation Day.

Part of the Christian backlash—I was assured by friends—was their opposition to local governments issuing demands for Cathy to retract his statements or threaten Chick-Fil-A's business dealings in the community. Thousands of Christians lined up to buy and eat chicken sandwiches and waffle fries. No one can possibly account for the motivations of thousands of people. What can be accounted for are the dollars earned by Cathy and the harm done to our gay, lesbian, and transgender friends.

I lived in a small community. I can't imagine what an LGBTQ student, working at Chick-Fil-A, might have thought when his Christian teacher, counselor, coach, or principal walked in and ordered a chargrilled chicken sandwich that day. I can't help thinking about what gay neighbors felt when families hopped out of their minivans and SUVs determined to "eat more chikin."

Was the peace of Christ extended that day?

People outside the church stayed outside the church. But somehow, some Christians believed a victory was won. We won!

People looking for victories are people looking for fights.

A Church at War

Romans, not to mention the teachings of Jesus, aren't interested in cultural prominence and certainly not dominance. The Bible pushes back on our desire to prop up a nation that ostensibly calls itself Christian while simultaneously denying the gentle, non-coercive spirit of Jesus. We can't have ceaseless fights to win and be people of living in harmony. Paul is interested in peace. "As far as it depends on us, live peaceably—or at peace—with all," he writes in Romans 12. Just when we get all settled with the idea of living at peace with our friends, family, and other folks who think like us, the folks the Homogenous Unit Principle seeks to connect us even more deeply with, Paul brings up that pesky word again: *all*.

Gazing across the Christian landscape we should not be surprised to discover that non-Christians are shocked to discover the Apostle Paul urged Christians to live in peace in the first place. So much of what we spend our time listening to and talking about bathes itself in the language of war. We are victims of the discourse. Listen to our popular language: "We've got a battle for hearts and minds. Can you help me out? I'm talking with an Atheist friend and I need some good ammunition. We need to stand up against the War on Christmas and the War on Christians. We've got a War on Terror and a War on Drugs. We've even got 'Worship Wars.'" Christians are fighting a cultural cold war and there is no shortage of enemies.

Christian bookstore shelves reflect—and may encourage—our reflex for aggression. Popular titles include *The Invisible War*; *Winning the Values War in a Changing Culture*; *The Culture Wars*; *Battle Ready*; *The Hardcore*

Battle Plan; When the Enemy Strikes; True Jihad; The Truth War; Every Man's Battle; Every Woman's Battle; Every Young Man's Battle; Every Young Woman's Battle; and *Financial Armageddon!* A library this combative can't help but coach her readers to view everything through the lens of hostility. Is there any meaningful way we can legitimately call ourselves people of peace if we're always spoiling for a fight? I frequently wonder how we got from "live peaceably with all" to our common pronouncements of war.

Fighting is easy. It just looks tough. It sounds like standing up for the gospel and not being ashamed, but it may be little more than fear of forces we can neither control nor explain. Even through all the scrapes and shouts, fighting is considerably easier to manage than peace. In our modern era, we don't have to wait until we see the whites of our enemies' eyes. The battlefields where we contend are cable news and AM radio—of both the Left and Right variety. We're armed with blog comments and rapid-fire e-mail forwards designed to dismember. In the twenty-first century, fighting is emotionally uncomplicated because when we fight we don't have to see faces. And perhaps because we lack sight to see faces we've lost God's vision for peace.

Until We See Faces

There are some faces I can never forget. I can never forget the face of my mother's friend, Joe. In part, I can't forget Joe because of a memorable and important gift he gave me nearly twenty-five years ago. At fifteen years old, I was a sophomore at Stone Mountain High School in Stone Mountain, Georgia. There are three crucial details everyone in the world needs to know about Stone Mountain. First is that Stone Mountain is a Gigantic. Stone. Mountain. The second detail concerning Stone Mountain is that Martin Luther King Jr. names Stone Mountain in his "I Have a Dream" speech. During the Civil War, Stone Mountain was used as an armory for the confederacy and later became a rallying point for the Ku Klux Klan. The third and most important detail—at least to me—about Stone Mountain is that while I was in high school, we had the number-one jazz band in the state and I was in it. As a matter of fact, we were one of the best high school jazz bands in the country, which gave us incredible opportunities. One of those opportunities emerged my sophomore year when we had the opportunity to tour Europe and play The North Sea Jazz Festival in Amsterdam and The Montreux Jazz Festival in Switzerland.

Both jazz festivals are huge. They were really festivals for all kinds of music; like SXSW for Europe. Artists like Stevie Ray Vaughn, Miles Davis, and Dizzie Gillespie played shows around the clock. Only I had a problem: we had to pay our own way. My parents were recently divorced, my brother had just started college at David Lipscomb University, and there was no way my family had the $5,000 to pony up for a trip to Europe. Even with all the fundraisers we were doing, I wasn't coming up with $5,000.

That's when Joe stepped in.

Joe had no children and had made a good living as an engineer. In a casual conversation with my mother, Joe said, "Gloria, this is what I'm going to do. I'll pay for Sean to go. I'll even give him spending money, because this is the opportunity of a lifetime."

Joe did pay. It was the opportunity of a lifetime.

If I had been my mother, I wouldn't have let me go. Think: twenty-two boys aged fifteen to eighteen cut loose in Amsterdam? Are you kidding? The red-light district. Nude beaches. No drinking age. No nightly curfew. A jazz band director who wasn't terribly interested in supervising us. There's no way I'd let my daughters go. In the end the trip was fine and we didn't get into too much trouble, but to this day I have a police record in Italy and may never step in that country again.

Other than that one little incident, we didn't get in too much trouble, but we did have a lot of fun. My friend, Wes, and I went to late-night jam sessions and soaked in the culture. Joe was right. It was the trip of a lifetime. And it was a trip I wouldn't have been able to take without the kindness of my mom's friend, Joe.

Joe was there for me when I had the opportunity of a lifetime. He was there for my mom when things were tough as she was navigating a divorce. Joe has been kinder to my mother than most people ever have been. He was always exceedingly kind to our family.

There is something you need to know about Joe. The reason Joe has no children is because Joe is gay. I tell you about Joe because we live in a culture and church that refuses to see Joe as a creation of God. On one side, we have a culture that says Joe is just a bag of impulses and he must and can only act from impulses and drives. And I know that's not true of Joe nor anyone else, regardless of the impulse. On the other side, I'm inundated with e-mail, newsfeeds, and media messages telling me that Joe is less than human and has an "agenda" and is trying to destroy my family. But it doesn't matter to me what your newsletter says, I know that's not true either.

I know it's not true of Joe or the several kids who are gay that grew up in my youth groups when I was a youth worker. I know it's not true of my wife's college friend who is also gay and whose Christian parents barely spoke to him for a number of years. In many ways, they too are victims of the discourse. For a decade and a half I was a youth minister. I took teenagers to Six Flags, to summer camps, on mission trips, to countless retreats and rallies, and I loved every minute of it—well, most every minute of it (I could have lived with better sleeping conditions on many of those retreats and mission trips). But I never complained because I always loved my kids. They were my kids. We shared our lives together. We joked. We cried. We served. We worshiped God. And we loved each other. I can't recount all the late-night conversations and heart-to-heart talks on long rides. Conversations about life and faith, God and evil, and the purpose of our existence peppered and seasoned my life as I walked alongside teenagers. They walked alongside me too.

Some of those teenagers are now ministers themselves—both inside and outside of churches. Some have adopted needy kids while they were still basically children themselves. Some of my kids have set out to change the world while others are just trying to hang on and save themselves. Some are therapists; others wait tables. They've become teachers and lawyers, accountants and musicians. Each one has chased God to the best of their limping abilities.

Some of those kids are gay.

These kids aren't celebrities "parading" their relationships in publications and in front of the cameras. They aren't activists working to bring disquiet to little old ladies carrying King James Bibles. They aren't shouters or screamers or dancing in the street. They never wanted to throw their identities into someone's face, like some of my Christian friends accuse them of.

These are my kids.

They have faces. And names. And stories. They have moms. And dads. And brothers. And sisters. They have hopes and fears. But mainly they want to live quiet, peaceful, and useful lives. My kids aren't stereotypes. They're not caricatures. They're flesh and blood; alive and kickin' people. They too are victims of the discourse, a discourse that has told Christian parents that the best way to redeem their LGBTQ children is to shun them and shut them out of their family.

Too many Christians have imagined biblical scenarios where Jesus shuns people. They must have imagined or made them up wholesale, because Jesus never shuns anyone. When we listen to the voices instructing us to behave in opposition to the ways Jesus behaved, we are quite literally listening to the voices of the anti-Christ.

One Night at Iftar

Elements in our culture tell us the same thing about Joe that they tell us about my friend, Abdur. When I lived in California and served as President of the Board of the Peninsula Clergy Association, which represented all the clergy of every faith, Abdur was on the board as well and served as our treasurer. Abdur was the local Imam. We became friends. I remember spending time holding Abdur's newborn baby and teaching one another about spiritual practices from each other's faith tradition. We frequently talked about our shared history in Abraham and the connection points within the three great monotheistic faiths—Judaism, Islam, and Christianity.

I met Abdur at the same time there was a ruckus about a group of Muslims building a community center two-blocks from Ground Zero in New York City. We shared Iftar together one night—which is the daily breaking of the Ramadan fast. He walked me around his congregation introducing me to members. They didn't seem like the people I kept hearing about on television. I could see in their eyes how hurt and exploited they felt about the words being said about them in the media, how misunderstood they felt, and worse, how they felt no one really cared to understand. But we live and move in an American Christianity that tells me I need to fight Joe and Abdur instead of striving to live at peace with them. And all they've ever been is kind to me.

I learned important lessons from Joe and Abdur. They showed me that people aren't caricatures. They are layered and deep. These people weren't the folks I saw being complained about and lambasted on the news. They had no "agenda" for the country. They never camped out in front of my house, picketed anyone's funeral, or threatened my family. They had only been good to my family.

We all know, at a personal and profound level that the people we're told to dislike and distrust aren't what we're told they are. You've been there. You have the experience of knowing the headlines and water-cooler talk aren't true. You know when the math doesn't add up? When the rhetoric doesn't meet the reality? You've been there when someone told you something about a person or a group of people and you knew—because you knew them personally—it wasn't true.

We've been told by supposedly "Christian" leaders that some folks are the enemy. They're dangerous. I've been told that about both gays and Muslims, but nothing about my actual life has ever suggested that was true. We are also told that to have a strong Christian witness requires us to be dismissive, argumentative, domineering, or exclusive to people, in my experience, who have only been kind to me.

The church has been lied to.

We've been told that having a strong Christian witness means certain behaviors at the ballot box, supporting particular and narrowly defined public policies, and eating at certain restaurants on certain days. We've suffered under a disinformation campaign convincing us that real and genuine Christianity is free to mock particular people, free to be cavalier about how we speak to others, free to name call, and free from guilt and blood when bombs and bullets reign down on innocent children if their parents bow in a temple rather than pray in a pew.

Most of all, we are lied to by the purveyors of power. They tell us that we can think and say anything as long as we are biblically accurate.

This has never been true.

This was the express problem Jesus had with the Pharisees. They were so concerned with the law—the law God himself had given—yet failed to understand that people were more important than the law. The Pharisees weren't wrong about the information. They were wrong about God. They were wrong about God's love for people.

As tempted as we are for conquest and control, the Scriptures call us to peace: "As far as it depends on us, live peaceably—or at peace—with all."

We can stash away our swords. We can put away our picket signs and stop sending almost-true e-mail forwards. We can stop spouting naked opinion as if it is fact across social media. We can turn off the talk radio and the cable news that is intentionally designed to keep us stirred up and angry.

When we choose peace instead of war we declare to the world: "I won't play your game. I won't do gay versus straight. I won't do black versus white. I won't do Red State versus Blue State. I won't do, 'I hope you fail.' I won't do male domination over female. I won't do love my neighbor and hate my enemy. I won't do rich oppression of the poor. I won't do disenfranchisement and marginalization. I won't do, 'Well, that's how they'd treat Christians in their country.'" Because while belligerence and antagonism may be the popular currency of a country that has turned America into a religion of it's own, the clear message of Paul is to live at peace.

Peace is Shalom, a state of wellbeing for all God's children. In the beginning, in the Garden, there was peace. In the New Heavens and the New Earth there will be peace. This is the peace Jesus invites us into every time we pray "May your will be done on earth as in Heaven." To speak peace is to announce a new kind of empire.

I don't get to choose the message. It's not my kingdom. And it's not yours either. And I know there are a lot of things we are tempted to say to our world, but Paul says to live in "peace."

As we've said, Romans isn't ultimately a letter about how we deal with our individual sin and guilt. Those were Martin Luther's questions and Martin Luther's answers, and Christians have been spinning around in his psyche for too long. We don't have to remain beholden to sixteenth-century questions and sixteenth-century answers. Romans is about how to create community between Jews and Gentiles, how to create community between two groups of people experiencing tension and suspicions, and the answer to that question harkens all the way back to what we discovered in Romans 3: "all have sinned and fall short of the glory of God."

Perhaps one of the more striking stories of finding peace is the story of Wilma Derksen. I discovered Wilma's story reading Malcolm Gladwell's book *David and Goliath*. Though Wilma tells her story around the world and has led and inspired millions, it was new to me. I spent two days reading about her story and what she went though. It formed, for me, a template for how to orient my life as a person of peace, even in the face of great loss and tragedy.

One afternoon, Wilma was at home, trying to clean up the family room in the basement, when her daughter, Candace, called. It was a Friday afternoon in November and that time of year in Canada the temperature was well below freezing.

Candace was thirteen. She wanted her mother to come pick her up from school. Wilma was busy that afternoon. The Derksens had one car. Wilma had to pick up her husband, Cliff, from work. She had two other children—a two-year-old and a nine-year-old. She would have to bundle them up, pick up Candace, and then go and pick up Cliff. It would be an hour in the car with three hungry children. There was a public bus. Candace was thirteen, no longer a child. The house was a mess.

Wilma asked Candace to ride home on the public bus.

Wilma went back to her housework. After about an hour, she stopped. Candace wasn't home yet, and it wasn't a terribly long walk. This was Canada and it was cold and snowing. The clock ticked. It was time for Wilma to go pick up her husband. She packed the other kids in the car, and drove slowly along Talbot Avenue, the road to Candace's school. She drove to the school. The doors were locked. No one could be found. They spotted a few other kids, but no one had seen Candace. Wilma went on to retrieve Cliff.

Immediately she told Cliff that Candace was missing and her anxiety was increasing. The family rushed back home and began calling Candace's friends. The last time anyone saw Candace she walking along Talbot Avenue. Wilma called the police. At eleven that night, two police officers knocked on their door and the officers asked them a series of questions about Candace's home life.

The Derksens formed a search committee, recruiting people from their church. They put up, "Have you seen Candace?" posters all over the city.

A month passed. No Candace. They took their two other kids to see the movie Pinocchio as a distraction, but the tale of Geppetto's lost boy was too much for Wilma and her aching heart.

Seven weeks after Candace Derksen's disappearance, the Derksens were at their local police station when the officers asked to speak to Cliff. After a few minutes, they took Wilma to the room where her husband was waiting and closed the door. "Wilma, they've found Candace."

Her body was found discarded in a shed a quarter of a mile from the Derksens' home. Her hands and feet had been tied. She had frozen to death.

Later, on the night the Derksens found out about Candace's death, they were visited by a man whose daughter had been killed a few years ago in a doughnut shop burglary. A man named Thomas Sophonow had been arrested for the killing and tried three times. He had served four years in prison before being released on appeal.

Wilma remembers their visitor going through all the trials—all three. She says, "He had this little black book—very much like a reporter does. He went through every detail. He even had the bills he'd paid. He lined them all up. He talked about Sophonow, the heartache of the trials, and his anger at the Canadian justice system.

He wanted to make something clear: This whole process had destroyed him. It had destroyed his family. He couldn't work anymore. He went through the medications he was on. I thought he was going to have a heart attack right there . . . He didn't talk much about his daughter. It was just this huge absorption with righteousness and justice. We could see it. He didn't have to tell us, we could see it. His constant refrain was, I'm telling you this to let you know what lies ahead."

The Derksens didn't want what this man had, a lifetime of emptiness, bitterness, and tears, all to never see his daughter again anyway. His life was a cautionary tale. He thought he was warning Cliff and Wilma. He was. He was showing them what it looks like to live in enmity.

The next day was Candace's funeral and the events were covered across all of Canada.

A reporter asked the Derksens, "How do you feel about whoever did this to Candace?"

Cliff responded, "We would like to know who the person or persons are so we could share, hopefully, a love that seems to be missing in these people's lives."

Over the years, the Derksens struggled to forgive. Eventually, Candace's killer was arrested and the Derksens were ultimately able to extend grace to him.

When asked how they were able to forgive and move forward, Wilma pointed to her religious tradition. She said she was taught an alternative way to deal with the world.

"Sharing a love," as Cliff Derksen put it, is the center of the gospel.

How then do we deal with enemies and people of whom we are suspicious? How do we handle those on the other side of the aisle or who disagree with us? How do we deal with spouses or friends or children in tense and trying times? How do we deal with church folks or people at work that we struggle to love and understand? Those who hinder and harm us?

This is how: Disarm.

10

Unarmed Empire

If peace can only come through killing someone, then I don't want it.

—Hiro Mashima

G ROWING UP IN MISSISSIPPI, the most important thing in my world outside of church was baseball. My brother Richard and I played baseball at school, we played baseball in the backyard, we played baseball on traveling teams; we even played baseball in the house. That's the first time I've ever confessed that in public. So, Mom and Dad, all that stuff that was broken . . . that was Richard.

I'm not being arrogant when I tell you that my baseball teams were *really* good. Our teams played in invitational tournaments all across southern Mississippi. Some of the guys on the teams went on to become professional athletes. Some even played in the NFL and MLB. My friend Terrell Buckley played football at Florida State University, was an all-American, and left Florida State as their all-time leader in interceptions. He went on to become the youngest player in NFL history to return a punt for a touchdown, and, oh, yeah, he also won the Super Bowl with the Green Bay Packers. I sometimes feel bad for him. He never experienced the same level of success I have in becoming the preacher.

One of our childhood baseball tournaments stands out among the many. We were invited to play against most of the other first-place teams from different leagues in the area. The tournament was in a big city, which isn't saying much in Mississippi. Remember, a mall is all you need in Mississippi to be a big city. Our excitement was high.

What I remember most clearly is that out of all the teams in the tournament, one thing made our team different. All the other teams' players were all white and our team was all *not* white. And we were going to spend the weekend playing in a tournament to see which team was the best. This was one of those sporting events that was more than a sporting event. This was about more than bragging rights or carrying home a trophy. Like the Munich Olympics, this Little League baseball tournament was going to be about personhood and equality. The other teams weren't Hitler, but we all felt a little bit like Jesse Owens.

Before the first pitch was thrown there was a snag. In our Little League players were allowed to steal bases. So if you were on first, for instance, after the pitcher threw the ball you could take off and steal second base. We were great at it. Our team was fast. We could motor. In fact, my dad and his fellow coach, Wayne, had built our team around speed and timely hitting. But the team hosting the tournament didn't steal bases in their league. All the coaches, managers, and tournament directors got together to determine which set of rules to play by.

We could steal bases.

And we did! We ran the mess out of those teams. We were stealing bases at every chance. Some of the other teams weren't used to it, and we took full advantage of their inexperience. We crushed every team we played. The outcome of our games weren't even close. Other teams from other leagues stole bases, too, but none with our frequency and speed. By the end of the weekend, we found ourselves in the championship game. As the tournament thinned and the brackets narrowed down to the championship game, we were elated to discover we were playing for the trophy against the home team. This was their tournament, and we were going to beat them in their house!

But a funny thing happened on the way to the championship game.

An hour before the game, my dad was called into a meeting with the tournament directors. They told him that for the championship game they were making a rule change. Teams would no longer be able to steal bases.

The rules we had been playing under were no longer the rules.

Changing the Rules

Does it ever feel like someone has changed the rules on you? For many followers of Jesus, it feels like we are entering a new space, a territory that's unknown. Everywhere you look, it seems like the ground is shifting underneath our feet. And the reason the ground feels that way is because it's actually shifting. Fewer and fewer people are claiming any kind of Christian commitment. We're seeing fewer and fewer people attending churches on the weekends, and there are even Christian bloggers taking pot shots at Christians and the church. When we turn on the television it seems like faith really is under fire in ways that feel threatening. People whose intent has only been to serve God question what it means when previously restricted groups like gays and lesbians can get married and Christian photographers, florists, and bakers can be legally enjoined to participate by providing services or are forced to go out of business because of their refusal to do so. Daily headlines remind us that Islam is sweeping across the world in two alarming ways. First, Islam is growing in adherents and second, men and women with a gnarled interpretation of Islam use it as camouflage to spread fear, hate, and their maniacal doomsday fantasies. All of this makes some Christians want to fight back. And fight back hard.

Some of us want to stand up and say, "Hey, America is a Christian nation! We're the home team! Shouldn't we get to make the rules?" Though I personally don't share the anxiety and angst of some of my brothers and sisters, I intellectually understand where they are coming from. When they look at America, as we discussed about American exceptionalism, they imagine Reagan's "city on a hill." Their parents, grandparents, and great-grandparents killed enemies and spilled their own blood in wars to maintain a country they love and they see much of that slipping away. Though amorphous and left intentionally vague, when these believers read America's founding mothers and fathers, they see references to God and interpret those references to mean the God of contemporary American Evangelicalism.[1] They believe Christians ought to be able to make the rules.

Jesus disagrees. Jesus doesn't actually think top-down positional power is the best way to announce God's kingdom.

In the Gospel of Luke, as Jesus prepares to send his disciples into the world on their own, he gives them explicit instructions about how to deal with an oppositional culture. He tells them,

> The Lord then recruited and deployed 70 more disciples. He sent them ahead, in teams of two, to visit all the towns and settlements between them and Jerusalem. This is what He ordered.

1. See Meacham, *American Gospel*.

Jesus: There's a great harvest waiting in the fields, but there aren't many good workers to harvest it. Pray that the Harvest Master will send out good workers to the fields.

It's time for you 70 to go. I'm sending you out *armed with vulnerability,* like lambs walking into a pack of wolves. Don't bring a wallet. Don't carry a backpack. I don't even want you to wear sandals. Walk along *barefoot, quietly,* without stopping for small talk. When you enter a house seeking lodging, say, "Peace on this house!" If a child of peace—one who welcomes God's message of peace—is there, your peace will rest on him. If not, don't worry; nothing is wasted. Stay where you're welcomed. *Become part of the family,* eating and drinking whatever they give you. You're My workers, and you deserve to be cared for. Again, don't go from house to house, but settle down in a town and eat whatever they serve you. Heal the sick and say to the townspeople, "The kingdom of God has come near to you."

Of course, not every town will welcome you. If you're rejected, walk through the streets and say, "*We're leaving this town.* We'll wipe off the dust that clings to our feet in protest against you. But even so, know this: the kingdom of God has come near." I tell you the truth, on *judgment* day, Sodom will have an easier time of it than the town *that rejects My messengers.* (Luke 10:1–12 The Voice)

I can only imagine the conversations around the campfire as Jesus gives these marching orders.

"This is great. We're going to change the world."

"You're sending seventy of us out, Jesus. What are we gonna call this thing?"

"How about Mission 70?"

"No, I got one. 'I Like Ike . . . and Jacob . . . and Joseph.'"

"No. How about 'Let's Take Jerusalem Back'?"

"No, that's terrible. Let's call it 'Missional Mercenary Mavericks' or 'Mighty Missional Men' or 'Unconditional Missional.' I don't know Jesus, I'm just spit-balling here, but let's stick 'missional' in there to make sure people know we're serious."

"No," Jesus says. "I've got a better name for what we're doing: Lambs Among Wolves."

"Lambs among wolves" doesn't sound quite right, does it? It doesn't sound triumphant or enthusiastic. It doesn't sound like something you could put on a bumper sticker. There's no hope and change. There's no

"Make Jerusalem Great Again." There's no "I'm with him." All the same, Jesus sends his first disciples out like lambs among wolves, armed only with vulnerability. And this is where anyone with any sense has to question Jesus's sanity. These are strange instructions. Why no wallet? Why no backpack? Why no sandals? What if someone steps on a rusty nail? I think we all know that's tetanus waiting to happen. Why in the world would Jesus send his disciples into the midst of wolves so utterly unguarded? So open to attack?

As we ask the question we can already hear the answer. There is something so deeply misaligned in the human heart and Jesus knows that unless his disciples go into the world unarmed they will fall into the temptation to stand their ground. We really do want to believe we are the home team and the advantage should be ours. We have forgotten what C. S. Lewis said, that we live in "enemy occupied territory." The fact of our moment in history is that in order to be faithful disciples of Jesus, we have to acknowledge the reality that we are dependent on the hospitality of the world and not the other way around. As Jesus sends out the seventy, he leaves them with no illusions: "Of course, not every town will welcome you." Rejection is baked into the cake. It's expected. It's standard. We don't get to make up the rules as we go. We don't get to dominate and enforce. We don't get to run things our way. To expect otherwise is to dismiss the guidance of Jesus and presume to know more than he knows. Or worse, to anticipate universal, or even widespread, acceptance reveals we don't mind being Jesus's emissaries as long as it involves little to no suffering. Perhaps we have fooled ourselves into believing that our country and our world are preparing themselves to rejoice at our arrival. It may be true that some populations will receive Christians as liberators, but we're silly if we think ready compliance with the gospel is owed to us. Therefore, each of us must come to terms with the way we interact with the world. We are not the home team. We don't get to make up the rules. Jesus wants us to know what's waiting on the other side of our front door.

Jesus gives us a more humble way of engaging the world. We enter the world unarmed. The reason we release command and control is because that's the way Jesus said to do it. Humility is the way of Jesus. As the disciples begin teaching and preaching the message of Jesus, the only word our Lord gives them is "peace." Christians are to proclaim peace.

Finding Our Way

When our family lived in California, our closest friends were a couple who hadn't been to church very much in their married life. Because of them, Rochelle and I began to see the world, the church, and the gospel in a new light. Our friends asked questions we'd never asked before and weren't satisfied with answers that satisfied us. We liked them and they liked us. Our kids went to school together, and soon they started worshiping with us.

The best aspect of having non-Christian friends is they have other non-Christian friends. Once you free yourself from gated Christian communities you realize that Jesus was right about the great harvest. Soon, our friends began telling their friends about their new friend who was a preacher. Lines were drawn immediately. They lost friends and people they'd known for years became suspicious of them. One night they had dinner with another couple from our daughter's school, Bill and Susan. Over the course of the night Susan peppered them with questions. "Well, Sean? What does he preach about equality? About homosexuality? About abortion? Those Christians" Susan stated, "are so backward and mean."

Trust me, I know Susan. The Christianity she knows is the Christianity of anger and exclusion. Susan knows the Christianity she's seen on television, a Christianity that seemingly always is at odds with progress, denies nearly universal scientific knowledge as fact, and is trying to convince Americans of the misguided notion that the family idealism of *Leave It to Beaver* actually existed. Christianity appeared to be bent on oppressing the LGBTQ community, and frequently on the side of big business and aligned against women, minorities, and the poor. In her view, if you were looking for a group of people attempting to discriminate and mask their discrimination under the cloak of religious freedom, it's Christians. She didn't want herself or her friends to be within ten city blocks of that kind of religion. Just the thought of it disgusted her. Regardless of what you might think of her, what is clear is that if Christians are going to talk about Jesus with people like her, we need different approaches than reflexively referring to America's past glory or expecting the world to defer to a Christian version of a set of particular ethics. It doesn't really matter if we want to blame the media or a few poor national spokespersons for the negative perceptions of Christianity; perception is reality and Jesus is still sending us out into to world.

Suspicion of the Christian faith is endemic to our cultural geography. There is no escaping it. In response, some of us have redoubled our efforts and entrenched ourselves in opposition to any cultural change. We've become more hard-edged, more concrete about doctrine and the "old paths." "We're going to stand up and fight," we say. "If you don't stand for something, you'll fall for anything," Christians warn. The mere appearance of the marginalization of cultural Christianity or the erosion of Christian dominance as reflexive in American politics and culture is cause for a counterattack. We've conflated contending for the faith with being contentious for the faith. Others of us have thrown out the baby with the bath water and determined not to believe very much at all. In an attempt never to say anything declarative (and thus be divisive), they've decided the most spiritual act on the planet is asking questions. "What do you think? How do you feel about that?" Still more of us have said, "There has to be a third way." Even on an elevator, some of us would look for a third way, but, if we're looking for a third way, that should signal to us that we've lost our way. Perhaps we should take Jesus at his word and try peace.

Disarmament

Our problem is that we don't believe peace is effective. Peace, for all the good we see in it, is a secondary concern for contemporary Christians, finding itself somewhere down the list after our safety, security, and the continuance of the American way of life. We don't like peace nearly as much as we relish protection. For instance, a 2014 *Washington Post*/ABC News poll found that white evangelicals largely supported the CIA's treatment of detainees (read: enhanced interrogation techniques such as waterboarding). Writing for *Religion Dispatches*, Sarah Posner reports that "sixty-nine percent of white evangelicals believe the CIA treatment was justified, compared to just 20% who said it was not."[2] It's unfair to draw a straight line from Christians' support of the CIA's tactics and a disregard for peace, but at the least, too many Americans view peace the same way the *Pax Romana* viewed peace, through power and control. Yet, that's not the way Jesus positions his disciples in the world. Jesus expects opposition from the world. He equally expects his followers to respond to that opposition with vulnerability. Jesus realizes not everyone is willing to accept the peace we extend. He says that's fine, move on, shake the dust off, and you know what, God will take care of the rest. God will take care of those who reject our offers of peace. There is never a need to respond to opposition with rancor. Armed empires

2. Posner, "Christians More Supportive of Torture than Non-religious Americans."

instinctively respond to opposition with force. And, perhaps, American Christians have learned to respond to aggression as an armed nation rather than an unarmed empire, dependent upon the hospitality of others.

Empires have predictable means of maintaining themselves, and those very means are corrosive temptations to the people of God. That is the exact reason God scolded Israel when they desired to be like other nations and have YHWH place a king to rule over them. The Lord tells them exactly what a king would require:

> Eternal One *(to Samuel)*: Listen to what the people are asking you to do. It is not a rejection of you—it is a rejection of My rule over them. It is what they have always done, from the day I brought them out of Egypt until today, rejecting Me and serving other gods. Now they are just doing it to you. So listen to what they are asking you to do, but make it plain to them what they are asking. Warn them about what will happen if a king is appointed to rule them.
>
> So Samuel told the people who were asking for a king what the Eternal One had said.
>
> Samuel: If a king rules over you, things will be different from now on. He will make your sons drive his chariots, be his horsemen, and go *into battle* ahead of his chariots. Your king will select commanders over 1,000 and commanders over 50. He will make some of you to plow his fields and collect his harvest; some of you will be *the blacksmiths* forging his shields and swords for battle and outfitting his chariots. He will force your daughters to make perfumes, to cook *his meals,* and to bake *his bread.* He will seize the choicest of your fields, vineyards, and olive orchards to give to his courtiers, and a tenth of your grain and your vineyards to give to his court eunuchs and servants. This king *you ask for* will take your slaves, male and female, *as his own* and put the choicest of your donkeys and your young men to do his work. He will take a tenth of your flocks. You will *essentially* become his slaves. One day you will cry for mercy from the Eternal One *to save you* from this king you have chosen for yourselves, but *be assured,* He will not hear you on that day.
>
> People of Israel *(ignoring Samuel)*: We have decided that we will have a king who will rule over us so that we will be like all other nations and will have someone to judge us and to lead us into battle. (1 Sam 8:7–20 The Voice)

The organizing principle of nations is self-preservation. Instead of trusting in YHWH to preserve Israel, the Hebrews want another Hebrew to get the job. This means human protection by human means. What's more, the larger and more expansive the empire becomes, the more it has to protect. Relying on human means greatly decreases the power and possibility of peace as a solution. Enmity becomes much more likely. Henri Nouwen captures the destructive nature of power well:

> The temptation to consider power a useful instrument of the proclamation of the Gospel is the greatest of all. We keep hearing from others, as well as saying to ourselves, that having power—provided it is used in the service of God and your fellow human beings—is a good thing.
>
> With this rationalization, crusades took place; inquisitions were organized; Indians were enslaved; positions of great influence were desired; episcopal palaces, splendid cathedrals, and opulent seminaries were built; and much moral manipulation of conscience was engaged in. Every time we see a major crisis in the history of the Church, such as the great schism of the tenth century, the Reformation of the sixteenth century, or the immense secularization of the twentieth century, we always see that a major cause of rupture is the power exercised by those who claim to be followers of the poor and powerless Jesus.[3]

As we saw in the story of Cain and Abel in chapter 2, differences have a way of devolving into violence. This was the way the *Pax Romana* saw the world, as well. This is why Jesus prescribes a new kind of engagement with the world. Brian Walsh and Sylvia Keesmaat describe the priorities of empires. "Empires always guarantee the status quo of privilege and oppression through a centralization of power . . . . Rome was renowned for its efficient military structure. Once a land had been conquered by Roman might, once the soldiers had taken their plunder and the garrison set up (which continued such plunder), the conquered area had to be made profitable for Rome."[4]

Empires, as the world has always known them, are propped up by inequality and force, but this is not how Jesus sounds when he releases his disciples to create a new community he calls the Kingdom (empire) of God. Jesus is aware of the very real and undeniable truth that rejection is central to the in-breaking of the Kingdom of God. He instructs his disciples to enter a dangerous world completely unarmed, as lambs among wolves. They are not even to return aggression for aggression. This

3. Nouwen, *In the Name of Jesus.*
4. Walsh and Keemaat, *Colossians Remixed*, 58–60.

simple but clear teaching of Jesus lies at odds in a church and world bent on cultural conquest. In a beautifully subversive way, Jesus knows what the rules of the world are (peace brought at the end of a sword) and roots his disciples in a different kind of orientation—unarmed and proclaiming peace. And Jesus is not merely making a one-time grounding in nonviolence, as if it were merely a tactic. There is a basic posture of power Jesus rejects. On the night Jesus is betrayed, the Lord is presented with the options of violence and the power dynamic of the world that boils influence down to coercion and force. Luke tells us, "When those who were around him saw what was coming, they asked, 'Lord, should we strike with the sword?' Then one of them struck the slave of the high priest and cut off his right ear. But Jesus said, 'No more of this!' And he touched his ear and healed him. Then Jesus said to the chief priests, the officers of the temple police, and the elders who had come for him, 'Have you come out with swords and clubs as if I were a bandit'?" (Luke 22:49–52). Jesus simply never advocates threatening, intimidation, or duress.

This is the moment where all we've seen above regarding Israel's story, contemporary political discourse, religious superiority, grace, Jew and Gentile relations, and choosing sides comes together. A church that comes to see control, intimidation, domination, force, or the use of political power as a legitimate means to reach God's end of love of God and love of neighbor is as far removed from God's preferred future as was the Roman Empire and every other empire that believed peace could be attained by domination. Even a cursory reading of the Scriptures, from Egypt, who enslaved the Hebrews because of their rising numbers, to the Roman Empire and their *Pax Romana*, reveals that God is not only opposed to these kinds of regimes but opposes them with power from his very hand. In Egypt, signs and wonders flowed from the staff of Moses. In Jerusalem, blood flowed from the hands of Jesus. Knowing this, churches ought to be conscious that methods of peace-making that are at odds with the loving-kindness of God not only tend to fail, but set God's heart against the seats of power from which they flow. A sure way to anger God is to lord power.

A Better Imagination

In the early twenty-first century, American Christians are faced with the very real—and perhaps natural—desire to choose means, methods, and peace-making tools of empires that have come before us. For instance, though an American living in the United States is more likely to die in a car accident than at the hands of an Islamic terrorist, it doesn't feel that way to many.[5] Add to that, governmental decay and terrorism in the Middle East creating a massive refugee crisis and the unavoidable result of Muslim men and women immigrating to Europe and to the United States. Many American Christians feel what terrorists want us to feel—terror. It is not surprising, given this emotional framework, to resist the teachings of Jesus and side with the power of empire. The best option, many believe, is to cut off the spigot, deepen our distrust of the Other, or fight fire with fire. Suggestions are made that Middle-Eastern refugees coming to the United States fill out questionaries. In France, Muslim women have been asked to disrobe from Burkas and Burkinos—bearing more skin—at public pools and beaches. In the midst of our disquiet about the remote dangers of terrorism, Christians, such as *Duck Dynasty* star Phil Robertson speaking of ISIS, can only imagine the postures of armed empires. Robertson, appearing on Fox News' *Hannity*, stated, "I'm just saying convert them or kill them—one or the other." Robertson's view of Christian engagement with the world echoes the methods of crusaders insisting Muslims or indigenous people be either baptized or drowned.

In the end, it may well be that Robertson is proven right. There exists in the world, as has always been the case, an intransigent evil that resists every effort at peacemaking, but what is *more* dangerous is that Christians have failed to inhabit the gospel of Jesus at a deep enough level that death is such an easy lever to pull. In the same way, Dr. Robert Jeffress, Pastor of First Baptist Dallas, responded to eight suicide bombers in Paris by calling for bombing as a response. To do so, Jeffress has to embrace a distinction between the Christian faith and democratic government that the Scriptures do not make. In a sermon addressing Islam and ISIS, Jeffress rightly called Christians to love, pray, and share the gospel. Then Jeffress makes a wild turn. He says that government is not required to love, forgive or turn the other cheek. On this point, we agree. The church and government have drastically different roles. Jeffress goes on to say that the government's responsibility is to safeguard her citizens. Then he makes an incredible intellectual leap. Because government is not called to love, forgive, or share the gospel, Jeffress then jumps from the Paris attacks all the way to his view that government's responsibility is to "secure the borders," though he never identifies what "securing the borders" means. There is somehow a

5. See Mueller, *Overblown.*

connection from forgiveness to borders? Continuing in this flurry of fear, Jeffress goes on to say "Borders are God's idea" and that "God doesn't mean for us to live all as one people." This is a dramatic, shocking, and wholly unbiblical idea. While a case can be made for strict citizenship inside a country, the belief that God is uninvested in us all being "one people" is dangerously false. It is, to put it bluntly, unbiblical from start to finish. To make matters worse, Jeffress goes on to commend Donald Trump's encouragement to "bomb the you know what out of ISIS" and "if we do not confront and defeat the evils of radical Islam, radical Islam is going to confront and defeat us." In the first five minutes of one sermon, Jeffress erases Paul's letter to the church in Ephesus. In fact, Paul's encouragement to the church on how to be the church (which is how to live Christianly in this world) is starkly at odds with what Jeffress preaches. Paul declares, "For he [Jesus] is our peace; in his flesh he has made both groups into one and has broken down the dividing wall, that is, the hostility between us" (Eph 2:14 NRSV). The very oneness Jeffress says God does not mean is precisely what God does mean and the cross of Jesus is proof. Timothy G. Gombis describes God's cosmic goal for humanity:

> God has acted to radically overturn the enslaving manipulations of the powers on a divided humanity . . . . The vision of the kingdom of God includes and celebrates racial, ethnic, and gender differences. But no singular gender, ethnicity or race is any close to God than any other . . . . In the death and resurrection of Jesus, therefore, God has triumphed over the fallen powers that run the present evil age. God has set Jesus Christ over them as cosmic Lord, and he is demonstrating his supremacy by freeing people from their enslaving grip and subverting their destructive aims of setting groups within humanity against each other.[6]

That Sunday morning in November 2015, Robert Jeffress abandoned his Bible and reached for empire. He discarded God's dream because he felt unsafe.

Both Robertson and Jeffress imagine a Christianity that is sheltered and protected by American military power. Even better, the imaginary wall they have created (when it suits their immediate political purposes) between governmental behavior and Christian personal behaviors is a soothing gel for the vulnerability they feel and are terrified of living. They want a Christianity that reflects the truths Jesus taught in the gospel, but only so

6. Gombis, *Drama of Ephesians*, 102–3.

far as it doesn't cost them what they want more—life and prosperity assured by tank and torture. It's fine for Jesus to die at the hands of corrupt powers, they just don't want to be like him.

People like Robertson and Jeffress want to live in an armed empire, not because they are mean or blood-thirsty, but because lamb-like living is vulnerable and sacrificial, virtues that have never co-existed with empire. Living as a lamb is, by default, to live exposed and defenseless and the church, along with our fellow Americans, has adopted a kill-or-be-killed philosophy. A combative orientation to the Other—whether they be ISIS or other forces of marginalization and death—cannot be harmonized with a Savior who explicitly teaches that we are lambs among wolves. Death, as difficult, foreboding, and unwanted as it may be, is the risk we take of entering the world in Jesus's name. We are not afforded the opportunity to be wolves among lambs, or, as is more likely the case with terrorists, even wolves among wolves. Because the crowds approach Jesus in the garden with swords drawn is not cause to draw swords in response. The uncomfortable truth of following Jesus is that for our Lord, the Apostle Paul, and millions of others throughout the years, death may be our last, best witness testifying to the love of Jesus.

Lambs among wolves is the posture by which we declare the gospel. The disciples seek men and women of peace and when none are found, they move on in peace. Too many in the modern church set out in Jesus's name to be his ambassadors but when we fail to find people of peace, our imaginations are limited to either conversion or death. This intoxication with force has even led many Christians to describe their engagement with the cultural forces opposed to their vision of the future as "culture wars." Somewhere near the root of this kind of thinking is amnesia. Those of us who are safeguarded by violence against foreigners abroad or anti-Christian forces at home have forgotten the Hebrews writer's admonition to "pursue peace with everyone, and the holiness without which no one will see the Lord" (Heb 12:14). And the church is worse for it. We've lost the connection between pursuing peace and seeing the Lord.

This fervor for fighting is contrary to the counter-culture spirit of love, harmony, brotherhood, and peace with which Jesus sends his disciples into the world. Christians are now faced with the simple decision of whether we choose to trust that God's people will be fed, led, and empowered by the same spirit that led the initial seventy or whether we are more comforted by the same mechanisms that empowered Egypt, Rome, and other long-expired empires.

It is now, at this very moment, that Christians worldwide need to recapture the vitality of speaking peace. Can we speak peace to our gay and lesbian neighbors? Can we speak peace to Republican, Democrats, Libertarians, or the Green Party when our visions of human flourishing may be wildly at odds? Can we speak peace to Islam or Buddhism or Mormonism as they absorb more and more territory around the world and inside the United States? Can we speak peace to the foreigner, the widow, and the orphan? Are we willing to be as vulnerable as lambs? Do we believe the Kingdom of God is strong enough that lambs can speak peace among wolves?

As Jesus's disciples return from their adventures in Luke 10, they share remarkable outcomes that are difficult to believe. They report, "Lord, in your name even the demons submit to us!" (Luke 10:17b). But Jesus, even though much has been accomplished in his name and through his empowerment, is less enamored with the disciples' success than they are. Where we might expect Jesus to rejoice in their achievements, he says, "Nevertheless, do not rejoice at this, that the spirits submit to you, but rejoice that your names are written in heaven" (Luke 10:20 NRSV). What matters to Jesus is not that his disciples can tread on snakes and scorpions, not that they can feel secure when facing existential dangers. He doesn't care that his followers can demonstrate power. He cares that they are in relationship with God in such a way that they reject false, armed security and embrace a deeper, eternal security.

In Romans, Paul connects peace and suffering. "Therefore, since we are justified by faith, we have peace with God through our Lord Jesus Christ, through whom we have obtained access to this grace in which we stand; and we boast in our hope of sharing the glory of God. And not only that, but we also boast in our sufferings, knowing that suffering produces endurance" (Rom 5:1–3 NRSV). Because we experience depths of peace with God, suffering is a cause for boasting. Like Jesus, Paul expects suffering at the hands of the world, but unlike us, sufferings provide an opportunity to boast. Paul knows what Jesus taught the seventy: When you are deeply secure in God, there is nothing left to fear.

I Had You the Whole Time

One summer while my daughters were still very little, my wife tore her left Achilles. I was a youth pastor at the time, so since my wife could barely stand, both my daughters were subjected to multiple youth trips. After a while, we were exhausted, and I begged out of our junior high camp, but I still had to drive the church kids to Abilene, Texas, from Houston. While I left Katharine, who was just a baby at the time, with my mother-in-law, my oldest daughter, Malia, traveled to camp with me to drop off our crew, spend the night, and drive home the next morning.

Malia was three years old, and more than anything she wanted to swim in the hotel pool. Hotel swimming pools are the French Riviera to kids, and although Malia had had swimming lessons she wasn't quite competing to be the next Katie Ledecky. We checked into the hotel, put on our bathing suits, went down to the pool, and dove in. We had the entire place to ourselves. She splashed and jumped and played, all with her in my faithful arms, until I decided to see what she could do on her own. I let her go, but just a little.

She did great.

Nothing could stop her jumping and splashing, until she realized my hands were absent. She panicked and began screaming. I reached out and grabbed her. She wrapped her arms around my neck, nearly choking me.

"Daddy, you saved me!" she blurted.

Inside I whispered, "Oh, sweetheart, I had you the whole time."

She never had anything to fear.

We are so unaccustomed to vulnerability that our natural reaction to feeling it is often panic and screams. We are tempted by methods of kingdom building that are engines of empire not devices of deliverances. Like Israel, we may ask for earthly, tangible means of protection that in themselves are a rejection of God. When the church embraces a *Pax Americana*, we deny and curtail the spiritual dynamism that Jesus gives to his disciples. Christians are kingdom dwellers, not guardians of an empire. Empires fear their extinction. Christians don't. We've been safe the whole time.

11

Methodological Kindness

He who sows courtesy reaps friendship, and he who plants
kindness gathers love.

—St. Basil

I T WAS JUNE 7ᵀᴴ, 1964. They had all gathered at the local Methodist church
like always. The meeting was another one of their regular get-togethers.
As usual they started with a prayer. Of course, they prayed. They were God's
chosen people. There was no doubting it. they were saved by Jesus to bless
the world. But on this particular night, someone wrote down the opening
prayer. The preacher, Sam Bowers, opened them with prayer: "Oh God, our
Heavenly Guide, as finite creatures of time and as dependent creatures of
Thine, we acknowledge Thee as our sovereign Lord. Permit freedom and
the joys thereof to forever reign throughout our land . . . May the sweet cup
of brotherly fraternity ever be ours to enjoy and build within us that kindred spirit which will keep us unified and Strong. Engender within us that
wisdom kindred to honorable decisions and the Godly work. By the power
of Thy infinite spirit and the energizing virtue therein, ever keep before us
our . . . pledges of righteousness. Bless us now in this assembly that we may
honor Thee in all things, we pray in the name of Christ, our blessed Savior.
Amen." And then the members of the Ku Klux Klan said "Amen," got up,
and started planning how to carry out "God's goal" for white supremacy.

Sam Bowers was a member of the White Knights of the Ku Klux Klan
in Mississippi and would eventually spend a good portion of his life in prison, though not as much as he should have. After their meeting dismissed,
the members of the Ku Klux Klan left, armed to the teeth with shotguns

and rope to fight against the civil rights movement that was "invading Mississippi," and within a few days, three civil rights workers were killed. Bowers served only six years for the murder of Andrew Goodman, Michael Schwerner, and James Chaney in 1964. Like Byron De La Beckwith, Bowers believed his actions were aligned with the will of God.

Bowers is not the first madman to believe he was seeking God's will only to invest the energy of his life, not in faith, hope, and love, but in pain, despair, and death. Part of the dysfunction, as we noted in chapter 8, is the failure of the church to understand the call of Jesus to befriend and love Others, but this is a corporate failure, a massive failure. On a more personal level, the De La Beckwiths and Bowers of the world are emblematic of a failure of Christians to disciple ourselves to the tutelage of Jesus. Certainly, distortions of the gospel such as the Homogenous Unit Principle shoulder their share of the blame, but their existence cannot be untethered from the church's and individual Christians' inability to know how personal piety and spiritual formation assist in creating unarmed empires. In short, men like Sam Bowers are fueled by a combination of the Christian community's unwillingness to call us out of our false selves, but also by our own opposition to develop as spiritual beings. This is how groups like Westboro Baptist Church—which routinely pickets the funerals of U.S. soldiers while carrying signs that read "GOD HATES FAGS"—are able to view themselves as thoroughly Christian, yet fail to demonstrate the character of Jesus. Instead of loving their neighbors, they create enemies of those near and far who dare offend them by not choosing their way of life and belief system as normative. At root is a misunderstanding about what God is up to in the world. Their concept—as best I can tell—is that men and women around the world serve and love God best by a strict adherence to a strict set of theological propositions. We might call this adherence to propositions "mental assent." Faith then becomes holding certain opinions about particular issues. Mental assent is followed closely by a corresponding set of public actions—voting, dating, marriage, religious practices, and other markers of righteousness. These are not unlike the acts of righteousness Paul undresses as meaningless throughout Romans. Frequently, inside the same communities, sins like physical abuse and sexual misconduct abound, but are minimized as long as those committing those sins hold steadfastly to the sacrosanct theological presuppositions (think well-known Christian leaders who are caught in sexual mishaps or theft, but return to ordained church leadership relatively quickly). What strikes me about men like Byron

De La Beckwith, Sam Bowers, the members of Westboro Baptist Church, and many Christians who cannot see their own viciousness is that they read the same Scriptures as great men and women of peace and brotherhood such as St. Teresa of Calcutta, Óscar Romero, and countless Christian martyrs who sacrificed their own lives for the sake of extending hospitality to others. Examining their lives, the line of demarcation is not a public confession that Jesus is lord or a mental assent. The difference that produces transcendent living is that these women and men were themselves transformed by a lifestyle deeply embedded in spiritual practices. Without spiritual practices there is no Spirit-filled living. As Francis of Assisi said, "Sanctify yourself and you will sanctify society."

Jesus's parting words point the way. "Ceremonially wash them through baptism in the name of the *triune God*: Father, Son, and Holy Spirit. Then disciple them. *Form them in the practices and postures that* I have taught you, and show them how to follow the commands I have laid down for you" (Matt 28:18–20 The Voice). Jesus instructs his disciples to enroll people in the school of Jesus and spiritually form them in spiritual practices. This is the essence of discipleship. *Disciple* is a first-century word for student. The difference between those who bring violence and those who bring peace is their personal enrollment in Jesus's school and a lifelong dedication to his way of engaging the world. One of the great causes of the church's failure to be a center of brotherhood and hospitality is that we've equated Christianity with mental assent to theoretical principles. But mental assent is not what it means to be Christian. Christianity is not merely concerned with what we think, though that is important. To be the kind of person who is a part of the kind of church that reflects God's one new humanity requires a personal commitment to becoming like Jesus, not merely believing he existed.

Jesus School Dropouts

My brother, Richard, is three years older than I am. At Stone Mountain High School—where we both graduated—there was a fifteen-minute period at the beginning of the day called "homeroom." During homeroom teachers took daily attendance, school announcements were shared, and we'd say the Pledge of Allegiance. It didn't matter if you were in remedial, general, or honors classes, homeroom was assigned alphabetically. The only thing students in homeroom shared were similar last names. When Richard was in ninth grade there was a student named Stephen in his homeroom. Stephen was smart, artistic, and funny. Stephen's dad was an inventor and was the creative mind behind fast-food menu items nearly every American has tasted. But Stephen had no use for school. Everyday, he sat next to my brother in homeroom and after attendance was taken, he'd escape to the rear of our high school where the smokers' area was (yes, that existed in the late eighties), and would slip into the woods never returning to school. Three years later when I was in ninth grade, the same student who sat next to my brother, sat next to me. It was Stephen. Stephen had been in ninth grade for three years. Only during my year, I suppose from the embarrassment of being in homeroom with Richard and then three years later with Richard's little brother, Stephen finally decided to get his act together. He quit skipping school, probably because the smokers' area no longer existed, and finally starting attending classes. We moved up to the tenth grade together. After tenth grade, though, Stephen dropped out of school completely.

Stephen is the perfect example of what it means to never become a student. Sadly, Stephen only shortchanged himself and his future because Stephen did the same thing most high school kids do. He spent four years in high school. He showed up everyday. Most days he skipped. When he wasn't skipping school, he slept through class. He did four years at Stone Mountain High School just like I did. Three of those years he did the same things over and over and over again, but the reason he never progressed and the reason he doesn't have a high school diploma today is because he never became a student.

The same thing happens in the church. Having reduced Christianity to mental assent associated with a set of theoretical propositions, we have failed to become students of Jesus. We have ceased being practitioners of Jesus's lifestyle, which is the only power capable of transforming us into the loving, hospitable people Jesus imagined we would be if we did what he did. William Paulsell perfectly describes our distaste for becoming God's students even when we know that long-term, dedicated practice is the only way to be transformed. He writes: "Athletes, musicians, writers, scientists, and others progress in their fields because they are well-disciplined people. Unfortunately, there is a tendency to think that in matters of faith we should pray, meditate, and engage in other spiritual disciplines only when we feel like it."[1]

1. Paulsell, "Ways of Prayer," 40.

Practice Makes

To practice the habits that made Jesus patient, loving, sacrificial, and con-nected to God is the fruit of following God. Humans are products of our habits much more than we are products of our thoughts. But habits require work. Oftentimes when spiritual disciplines are discussed we repel them by arguing, "we're saved by grace, not by works," which is true. The problem, though, is that some well meaning people say, "We're saved by grace not by works," as if to say that since Jesus died on the cross we can lay back on the beach and sip lemonade. When we discourage spiritual development, we reveal something deeper and darker living inside our hearts. We unsus-pectingly reveal that we don't truly love God. We don't want to be nearer to God than we currently are. We don't want to know God anymore than we currently do. We just want to get what we can get. We want our relationship with God to be friends with benefits. Perhaps Dallas Willard speaks best to this objection. "Grace," Willard says, "is not opposed to effort. Grace is opposed to earning. Earning is an attitude. Effort is an action."[2] Most of us don't like the sound of "spiritual disciplines." We like the "spiritual" part, but not the "disciplines" part. Disciplines sound burdensome and overwhelm-ing. Very few people sign up for discipline. No kid comes to their parents and says, "Mom and Dad, I really need some discipline. You really should roll back this allowance you're giving me." Adults don't like it much either. We don't sign up for discipline. But that's the problem. We want to grow closer to God; to be more like Jesus, but we cannot do it without a certain and particular kind of dedicated interaction with God. Dallas Willard calls this intentional submission to the way of Jesus "training for reigning." He means that God is searching the world for the kind of men and women he can trust with great responsibility. Gary Black describes it clearly:

> The primary purpose for human life is that each of us can know and experience the unique and creative Spirit and power that pulsate within the life of God by willfully choosing to disciple ourselves to Christ . . . . He [God] is going to create a community of lov-ing, creative, intelligent, faithful, powerful human beings who will steward the earth on his behalf and through his empowerment. The question is not if; it's who. That's what this life, human life, and experience seek to unveil in purpose and by design. All of human history, including your history and mine, is moving toward the collection and development of *an all-inclusive circle of relational*

2. Willard, *The Great Omission*.

harmony where all created beings, including humans, engage with and enjoy God's infinite realm and existence, such that the gates of hell don't stand a chance.[3]

Willard and Black point to our failure to understand our lives as students of Jesus as the cause behind our inability to create all-inclusive circles of relational harmony. Therefore, those of us desirous of living, being, and inviting others into the church we dream of, have to reposition personal and communal spiritual formation to the center of our lives and the life of our churches. The church cannot become *an all-inclusive circle of relational harmony* if we fail to be disciples, both individually and corporately. Spiritual practices and the actions of communities of faith are inescapably linked. Christians and churches who do not practice spiritual disciplines cannot become communities of relational harmony.

The New Kind

So, what kind of spiritual disciplines might be most crucial for creating the kinds of open, hospitable churches God intends? Given our contemporary religious landscapes, and all we've said about the Christian temptation to see cultural engagement through the lens of war, perhaps the best place to start is by embracing the fruit of the Spirit, particularly kindness. Why kindness? First of all, the fruit of the Spirit is often misunderstood as nine separate virtues that Christians are either blessed with or free to develop independently if they choose to. But the fruit of the Spirit is not a class you can skip if you'd rather go out back and smoke. The fruit of the Spirit is the virtue that flourishes over time in the heart and character of people and communities dedicated to God's Kingdom. Perhaps a better way to envision the fruit of the Spirit—and it is one thing, one fruit, not multiple virtues—is as tentacles all connected to the same hub; a nine-armed octopus, where love, joy, peace, patience, kindness, goodness, faithful, gentleness, and self-control are each connected to one organism. Without the full complement of arms, the octopus ceases to be an octopus. One of the reasons the virtue of kindness might be a place for us to reframe Christians' engagement with culture rather than virtues like love, is because we do not talk much about kindness. It may be the aspect of the fruit of the Spirit that is least talked about and the least publicly displayed. Christians talk about love a lot, and

3. Black, *Preparing for Heaven*, 81–82; italics mine.

rightly so, but love and kindness have always walked hand in hand in God's story. Kindness, in many respects, gives us a road map for love. As Richard Beck has said, "Kindness is the tutor of love."

Kindness is central to who God is. There may be no word in the Old Testament that more powerfully describes God's heart toward God's people than *hesed*, which is translated loving-kindness, loyal love, kindness, mercy, or love. The problem with love is that it's become too slippery and shapeless. It means nearly everything and is used to sell everything from bath soaps to diet pills. When a word begins to mean everything, it means nothing. Add to that the fact love's indeterminate meaning abandons it to mean whatever the speaker wants it to mean. From the teenaged boy fumbling around the backseat of his mom's minivan trying to convince his girlfriend of his pure intentions, to picket sign holders protesting whatever the latest headlines suggest they picket, we tell ourselves and others that we are doing whatever we are doing out of love. The measuring stick for love is the motives we assign to our behavior. Any conduct can be described as loving if we've convinced ourselves of it. Love has become a feeling using a singular diagnostic tool: how we feel. Kindness, however, defies our feelings. *Hesed*, God's loving-kindness, is not about our emotions. Kindness is about action, and more than that, loving-kindness is measured by how our actions impact the end-user. When God describes God's self, the description comes in terms of his loving-kindness in connection to God's behavior.

> Then the Eternal One passed before him.
> Eternal One: The Eternal God, full of compassion and mercy, slow to anger, and abundant in loyal love (*hesed*) and truth, who maintains loyal love (*hesed*) to thousands *of people*, who forgives wrongdoing, rebellion, and sin; yet does not allow sin to go unpunished, extending the consequences of a father's sin to his children, his grandchildren, and even to the third and fourth generations. (Exod 34:6–7 The Voice)

Even in the context of wrongdoing, sin, and rebellion, God's loving-kindness is at the center of God's interaction with humans. Kindness is enacted love, living and breathing in real time. When people are shown kindness they recognize what someone else has done on their behalf, not by what someone else felt. On an interpersonal level, we see the foreigner and widow Ruth give thanks to Boaz for his kindness toward her (Ruth 2). Joseph, the dream interpreter, asks the cupbearer, upon his release from prison, to show him kindness by mentioning Joseph to Pharaoh

(Gen 40:14). The Israelite spies show kindness to Rahab and her family for her assistance in taking the promised land (Josh 2:12–13). Of all the beautiful and grand words Christians associate with God, and though it appears in the Old Testament 246 times, we are far too slow to proclaim God's radical kindness. And our failure to do so has contributed greatly to our deficiency in practicing kindness toward our friends, neighbors, and enemies. We too easily get caught in a love loop, saying words and performing acts that are fundamentally about our feelings and calling them love regardless of their effects.

Unkind Speech

Job was a man who understood God's kindness. Job's friends, however, like many of us, ignored God's kindness and instead opted to argue theology rather than demonstrate kindness. You all remember Job's story. Satan makes a wager with God and Job is trapped in the middle. In a flash, Job loses his wife, his children, his wealth, and his health. We see Job in the Scriptures with shards of clay pots picking away his sores. His life is in ruins. Then Job's friends show up.

Initially, they are good friends. They sit with Job for seven days and don't say a word. (Most of my friends are preachers. There's no way they could not talk for seven days.) Then their silence breaks. Job's friend, Eliphaz, begins to speak into Job's life.

At first, Eliphaz's speech is courteous and gentle. He tells the group about a vision he's received. Eliphaz talks about a "tent-cord" which is an image for disaster that comes to the wicked. At the heart of Eliphaz's speech is a desire to make it easy for Job to repent. Before we throw stones at Eliphaz, we should consider that Eliphaz likely believed his motives were pure. When God's people see others behaving in ways that will hurt them and separate them from God, it's a good instinct to encourage them to rethink their choices and repent. That's a good thing. The flip side, though, is that many of us have boiled down the Christian faith to being Eliphaz whenever we can, regardless of context or knowledge. Our vocabulary has become pretty limited. One word: repent. It is not that repentance isn't needed and good, but there's always more to any story than the smooth, dualistic connections that reduce faithful living to mere repentance. In Eliphaz's world, a world based on the theology of Proverbs that was based on an if/then system of reward and punishment, Job has clearly sinned. Why else would

Job suffer? Eliphaz is doing decent theology when he talks with Job. Not only is he doing decent theology, he's doing it from his own feelings of love for Job. Eliphaz and his friends want the best for Job. His words come from a pure heart. Repentance is a good thing.

But repentance is not the only thing. Eliphaz demonstrates to us that we might need to keep quiet until we've heard the hurting and those who appear to be away from God tell their own story in their own words. Until we know what others have experienced, until we have heard what they say about their own experiences, we don't know enough to speak with any level of knowledge or credibility.

After Eliphaz's sermon, Job stipulates that he doesn't fully understand what's happening or comprehend why he's suffering. He'd rather be dead than in this situation. But Job isn't interested in his friend's pontification. Job turns to Eliphaz and says, "Anyone who withholds kindness from a friend forsakes the fear of the Almighty" (Job 6:14 NIV).

This is stunning. Job listened to his friends. He knows what they know about God and faith. They are reading from the same Bible, singing from the same hymnal. But for Job, to sit with the suffering and grieved and talk theology is staggeringly malicious. People who cannot sit with the distressed, those who fail to extend mercy to the pained, have not become students of their master Jesus. They visit criticism rather than extend mercy. They abandon the aims of God and forsake his loving-kindness. Job tells us exactly how a moralizing approach to others that is devoid of kindness hinders public witness.

> But my brothers are as undependable as intermittent streams,
>
> as the streams that overflow
>
> when darkened by thawing ice
>
> and swollen with melting snow,
>
> but that stop flowing in the dry season,
>
> and in the heat vanish from their channels. (Job 6:14–17 NIV)

Streams that stop flowing are not streams. They are dry beds—useless, and like the fig tree Jesus cursed, unable to perform the basic tasks for which God created it. Job says people armed with theology and lacking kindness are streams that in the summer, when most needed, are completely purposeless.

Is it possible that when we want to be theologically astute and doctrinally accurate the way Eliphaz wanted to explain God and repentance to Job, when we want to outline all the ways the Bible is calling people to repent, that when we fail to be kind, we fail to be useful as God's people? A Christianity that fails to speak and act with kindness is a failing stream. Dry streams can only tell stories about what it used to be like to move and bring life. They just aren't effective anymore.

Christians can be right, but if we are not kind, we are wrong.

Adding Injury to Injury

Several years ago Rochelle worked alongside a woman whose recent life had been so tragic it's almost hard to imagine. She was very much like Job. Rochelle was teaching seventh grade science at a large middle school when she heard the story of one of the sixth-grade math teachers, Cassandra. Six years before Rochelle and Cassandra met, Cassandra's daughter, Amy, had been diagnosed with a rare, deadly form of brain cancer. For years, Cassandra and her family lived in Arkansas near a chemical treatment plant that failed to adequately take care of their waste. Amy was diagnosed in April and died the following December. She was six years old. The following year, Cassandra's husband, Ron, was diagnosed with the same cancer. He died fifteen months after his diagnosis. Almost everyone who had lived in their old, Arkansas neighborhood lost someone to cancer. When Rochelle met Cassandra, her son was nineteen years old and had just received his cancer diagnosis. It was the same as his little sister's and his father's, and Cassandra began counting the days to his demise.

Cassandra and her family were Christians and had always been active in the local churches they attended. Her son's diagnosis, along with the unapologetic demands of teaching school, and the crippling grief of the prospect of losing another loved one to the same cancer, broke Cassandra in ways that are incomprehensible to most people. Cassandra shared her story at lunch with Rochelle and a group of teachers who were all believers. In the process, she shared how exhausted and broken she felt; how paralyzed by heartache all this had made her, and that for months now, years really, she had been angry with God. At the moment Cassandra was reaching and hoping for consolation, she was greeted by disapproval. One coworker after another responded to her cry for solace with judgment telling her how she shouldn't blame God and that she should really make it a point to get to church this Sunday. Some, out of loving motivations, invited her to their church. And they were largely right. In times of distress, too often people turn away from the resources most willing and able to aid them in their heal-ing. We often dismiss those able to come along side us and bear our burdens. But, like Eliphaz with Job, that's not the point. Cassandra didn't need a group of people to tell her to get her life straight, not during that moment. The point of a kindness-infused Christianity is to sit with people in their pain without criticizing either the cause of the pain nor their handling of it. Cassandra would have been deemed unspiritual or anti-Christian had she turned to her lunch group and said what Job said, "you have not been kind," but that would have been entirely appropriate. Their thimble-deep understanding of Christianity where everyone always paints-by-numbers and pain is met with platitudes only added injury to Cassandra's injuries.

The Fruit of the Spirit

The Apostle Paul says that kindness is a "fruit of the spirit," a marker that demonstrates that we are becoming the type of students to Jesus who take his teaching and example seriously. Kindness is not simply being nice, though that's a popular, but feckless, understanding of kindness. If we stop at niceties, we will end up with a faith that offers comfort, but rooted only in comfort. Rather, kindness is the posture of people who actually have the Spirit of God flowing in, through, and out of them. It is neither a state of mind nor an invisible attitude. Kindnesses is inextricably webbed to behavior. Therefore, as a spiritual practice it requires dedication and inten-tion and cannot be practiced by Christians who have not enrolled in the school of Jesus. There is nothing random about the kindness the Bible calls the church to practice.

In 1 Samuel we find the story of how David became king. If you're familiar with the Bible, you will recall that God called Saul to be the first King over Israel. And if you're really familiar with the Bible, you'll know that Saul's chief quality for King was that he was tall. But Saul fell out of fa-vor with God and God choose David, a shepherd boy, to replace Saul. This creates a problem. Saul is king, wants to stay king, and he wants his kingly line to continue through his son, Jonathan. David is not part of Saul's plan.

Saul is no fool. He has read *The Art of War* and knows to keep his friends close and his enemies even closer. He invites David to serve at the pleasure of the king, playing music to calm his nerves. What Saul hadn't counted on was that David and Jonathan would become friends. Worse for Saul, Jonathan recognizes God's favor on David and wants to honor God.

> Jonathan (to David): Let the Eternal God of Israel be my witness; this is my vow. When I have talked to my father, about this time tomorrow or no later than the third day, if he acts friendly about you, won't I send an answer to you? But if my father plans to harm you, then may the Eternal do to me what he plans for you—and more—if I don't let you know and send you away to safety.
>
> May the Eternal One be with you, as He has been with my father. If I live, then show to me the faithful love of the Eternal that I may not die. Do not ever take your faithful love away from my descendants, not even if the Eternal were to remove all the enemies of the house of David from the face of the earth.
>
> With these words, Jonathan made a covenant with David and his descendants. (1 Sam 20:12-16 The Voice)

Jonathan and David make a covenant. Jonathan will help David escape and David, in return, will be faithful to Jonathan's family. If you fast-forward the story, Jonathan does help David escape. David does become king and now David wants to fulfill his covenant.

> David: Is anyone from Saul's family still around that I could honor for the sake of my friend Jonathan?
>
> One servant from Saul's household, Ziba, was still alive, and they brought him to King David.
>
> David: Are you Ziba?
>
> Ziba: At your service, Majesty.
>
> David: Is anyone from Saul's family still alive to whom I could show the kindness of God? (2 Sam 9:1-3 The Voice)

This is critical. When it comes to kindness, David is not waiting to bump into an opportunity to be kind. He creates one. Again, kindness is deliberate.

For several years my oldest daughter, Malia, has been inspired by the story of Malala Yousafzai. Malala is a teenaged Pakistani advocate for women's rights and girls' access to education. On October 9, 2012, she was shot in the head during an attempted murder.

Malala was just fourteen years old when a Talib fighter boarded her bus, pointed a pistol at her head, and pulled the trigger. She survived and made a full recovery in England. Since that time, Malala has won the Nobel Prize for peace, been the subject of books and documentaries, and continues to be a transformative figure for human rights, particularly for women.

Even after being shot, Malala advocates for social rights and education in the face of continued threats against her life.

A few years ago Malala was a guest on *The Daily Show with Jon Stewart*. Her answer to one of Jon Stewart's questions stunned his audience. Stewart asked her how she reacted when she learned that the Taliban wanted her dead. Her answer was absolutely remarkable:

> I started thinking about that, and I used to think that the Talib would come, and he would just kill me. But then I said, "If he comes, what would you do Malala?" then I would reply to myself, "Malala, just take a shoe and hit him." But then I said, "If you hit a Talib with your shoe, then there would be no difference between you and the Talib. You must not treat others with cruelty and that much harshly, you must fight others but through peace and through dialogue and through education." Then I said I will tell him how important education is and that "I even want education for your children as well." And I will tell him, "That's what I want to tell you, now do what you want."[4]

Malala encapsulates one of the foundational attitudes for Christians dedicated to developing the spiritual practice of kindness when she says, "I even want education for your children as well." At the heart of kindness is a desire to treat others the way you want to be treated, to wish for others the same things you wish for you and your family and then behave in ways to produce it. This is why David seeks someone from Jonathan's family to be kind to. It is what he desires for himself. David knows the difference it makes to have someone show kindness. Kindness received leads to kindness extended.

What if we looked at one another and instead of being concerned about ourselves as individuals, we said, "What I want for me, I want for you." What if, in an effort to be an unarmed empire, we changed our attitude from "What's in it for me? What feeds me? What serves my interest?" and instead we said, "What I want for me, I want for you. Even if it costs me?" This is the nature of kindness, and it is the heart of Jesus's teaching to "do to others as you would have them do to you" (Luke 6:31).

No one I know wants to be shamed. No acquaintance of mine desires exclusion or subjugation through cultural or political power. My LGBTQ friends and neighbors have never signed up to be mocked, marginalized,

4. Acuna, "The Moment Nobel Peace Laureate Malala Yousafzai left Jon Stewart Speechless."

or denied services. The Hispanic women and men I lived among and ministered to along the border of South Texas have never desired being labeled rapists and degenerates simply because of their hunger for creating a better life for their children. My fellow African-Americans do not covet being told their lived experiences are overblown, made up, or, worse, that their lives don't matter. I want to be clear: Wanting for others what we want for ourselves is neither fanciful nor political. It is what we do when we become Jesus's students and are shaped into people who exhibit the full spectrum of the fruit of the Spirit. To be kind is not to be weak nor milquetoast about doctrine or theology. Loving-kindness is the essence of Jesus's doctrine and theology.

Interestingly, the Greek word for Christ is *christos* and the Greek word for kind is *chrestos*. In the early days of the new and forming Jesus movement, since *christos* and *chrestos* were so similar in sound and spelling, early followers of Jesus were often misidentified. Sometimes when people meant *christos* they said *chrestos*. Instead of being called Christians, they were called "the kind ones."

Wouldn't it be great if that were to happen again? Wouldn't it have been great if that was what Sam Bowers had prayed?

12

Drinking Real Wine

Holy Communion is offered to all, as surely as the living
Jesus Christ is for all, as surely as all of us are not divided
in him, but belong together as brothers and sisters, all of us
poor sinners, all of us rich through his mercy. Amen.

—Karl Barth, *Deliverance to the Captives*

S UNDAY NIGHT BAPTISMS WERE not uncommon in the church of my
childhood and adolescence. It was so common that I found Sunday
night, in a private gathering, the most appropriate time and place for my
own baptism. My tribe practices what we call "believer's baptism." Baptism
is typically spontaneous and immediate. We've always placed a great deal
of importance on people making their own, relatively informed decision to
follow Christ, which is symbolized through baptism. I understand that no
one truly knows all the connotations and commitments we take on when
we are baptized, but it seems reasonable to me to know a little of what those
commitments are. I also recognize the importance and blessing parents
who choose to baptize their infants are trying to pass on to their children.
Their argument for doing so has merit, but that's neither the way I was
raised nor my interpretation of what happens when men and women in
the New Testament are baptized. But my tribe's approach to baptism has its'
own demerits and foibles.

It was one of these Sunday night baptisms that brought this reality
to my mind. In the mid-1990s I was working as an intern for a midsized
church in San Antonio, Texas, and this was my first Sunday night. At the
end of the Sunday evening worship service, one of the junior high school

boys responded to the invitation song—something like "Just as I Am," I'm sure—by walking to the front of the worship center, sitting on the front row and whispering to the preacher his desire to be baptized. The boy was in sixth grade and looked even younger. This was my first youth ministry internship and I thought, "Wow! I must be amazing. My mere presence here this summer has already produced a baptism." This internship was for college credit, and I was definitely going to count this baptism in whatever metrics I would use to prove how awesome I was when I turned in my end-of-summer reflection paper. I soon realized that the story of this baptism wouldn't get within thirty city blocks of my summer review. I was embarrassed by it.

As that summer wore on, I never saw that newly baptized boy again. He was away at camps for a good portion of the summer, and turns out he and his family just weren't all that active in the life of the church. His dad traveled a great deal, leaving mom with more than a handful just dealing with life. I had supposed that, like my baptism when I was about his age, his would create a surge of spiritual aspiration, that it would be the catalyst for seriousness and fervency. It wasn't. And it wasn't because for all of our talk about believer's baptism, he never wanted to be baptized. He was forced to do it.

A few months after I returned to college, I got the full story of the Sunday night baptism. It seems that earlier that Sunday, at the end of service, the kid had sidled into the church kitchen and drank the leftover grape juice and crackers from the day's communion. Here's where it might be helpful to understand some of the idiosyncrasies of the church of my childhood. For many congregations, baptism and communion are necessarily connected. Only the baptized can take communion and only those baptized as "adults" and by immersion. In my tradition we share communion (Eucharist) every Sunday. It's a simple meal consisting of grape juice and a small cracker, which are passed to members as they're seated in their pews. Unfortunately, there's typically no liturgy or formality associated with communion. There's no blessing of the Host or consecration. Most of us see the bread and juice as symbolic. Or so we say. Since this young man had eaten the bread and juice from communion, his parents became uptight about his eternal destination. Not only does my tribe practice believer's baptism, many have long believed that the act of baptism is the point of contact between the human being and the saving act of Christ. It's with this sensitivity to baptism and communion that this young man's parents hurriedly called the preacher Sunday afternoon to talk to the boy about being baptized which then prompted the march forward Sunday night. The two went hand-in-hand. If he ate "communion," he needed to be baptized.

In the churches I've lived among, communion has mostly been an argument in thought and an afterthought in practice. That is to say, we talk a good game. We said that the Eucharist—interchangeably called "communion" or "the Lord's Supper"—was the reason we gathered together. Worship, in our rhetoric, was centered on table rather than proclamation of the Word or other acts of worship. We just didn't behave that way. Deacons, standing in the back of auditoriums, tested themselves by how fast communion could be served, and men—and only men—were routinely gathered for serving the elements about five minutes before services started each Sunday. There was nothing special about it other than to take it.

In my tribe, communion has often been a lever to get people to do what we really wanted them to do: be baptized. If parents know anything about kids it's that they like to eat. There are churches and Christian parents who request that kids not leave worship until "after communion" so that kids can see communion. Parents have also been charged with using their children's desire to snack against them. When they ask about having some bread and juice in worship, children are told—again, this is in my tradition, the unimmersed typically don't take communion—that they can eat it *after* they're baptized. You can imagine what happens. Many kids are baptized only in order to take communion. Their desire to fully participate in the community mandates a faith commitment.

What's evident in this thoughtless and manipulative approach to communion is a complete disregard for the dynamism, fellowship, and power to bring healing and hospitality that are inherent to the practice. Communion does not exist to give the church another rite of passage nor liturgical hoop to jump through. It's not designed to instruct the way a manual is. Communion is designed to teach us how to be together.

Because I could not find any explicit teaching instructing me that only baptized believers could take communion, Rochelle and I have always encouraged our daughters to participate fully in the life of the church. Just about every parent of young children in my congregation does the same. Add to that the fact that my daughters have always attended Episcopal schools and shared the Eucharist there (with real wine) since they were five, it seemed strange to allow it at school and not at church. I did have one caveat, though. In order to participate, I asked them both to read, recite, and eventually memorize 1 Corinthians 11:23–26, the Words of Institution. Each Sunday as we shared together, I'd open my Bible, have them read the words quietly, and I'd ask a few questions about what they thought it meant. Predictably, their answers reflected their levels of knowledge and maturity. One Sunday morning, our oldest daughter, Malia read the entire chapter. I'll always remember the look in her eyes and the horror she expressed when she asked, "Why were they mistreating the poor?"

At the heart of the Eucharist, Jesus and Paul give us a new way of being with one another. If taken seriously and impressed in the heart of the Christian church, communion has the power to transform the divisions that exist between people both in and outside the church. I know this first-hand.

The words, "You have to be $^$*%^*^* kidding me," were the first words that came to mind four years ago when I returned to visit a church where I used to work. We had ten, mostly good, years there, but the end didn't live up to the good times we shared. Three years before my return visit, while I was still ministering in that church, I went to a denominational gathering. When I left my house, I'd been serving my current church almost ten years. Two days after I came home, I was fired. My position "had been eliminated."

I was hurt and mad and I knew exactly who to be mad with. I suspected I knew which people in the leadership were behind my dismissal, and I wanted a measure of revenge. But I understood that there are pushes and pulls in life (and ministry), so I moved on, taking my heartache with me. I'm the kind of guy, though, who likes to beat the odds, prove others wrong, and make people regret their ill treatment of me. It's not the best part of me, but I can't act like it doesn't exist. So that's exactly what I'd planned on doing as I loaded my boxes and packed my bags. I would best my opposition one day and exact my revenge. I'd come out on top and have the last laugh. That church would regret this. If only in passing, I wanted someone, anyone, to think, "What a mistake we made." I'm told that most men think that when they've been cut loose, but I'm not proud that I did.

My problem was that I owned a Bible and at the heart of the biblical story is the death of Jesus and the celebration of Jesus's death, burial, and resurrection through the Eucharist. When you're disconnected from God's heart and Jesus's sacrifice, you really want church only to be about hymnals and pews and pulpits; you'd love for the center of the Christian faith to be doctrinal debates or church growth strategies, but it's not. The center of the faith are the Words of Institution that I required my daughters to learn.

Paul hands down a ritual to the church that he believes shapes the active life of the church.

> For I received from the Lord what I also handed on to you, that the Lord Jesus on the night when he was betrayed took a loaf of bread, and when he had given thanks, he broke it and said, "This is my body that is for you. Do this in remembrance of me." In the same way he took the cup also, after supper, saying, "This cup is the new covenant in my blood. Do this, as often as you drink it, in remembrance of me." For as often as you eat this bread and drink the cup, you proclaim the Lord's death until he comes. (1 Cor 11:23–26 NRSV)

Communion stands in continuity. Paul is passing on what he has learned to the churches he is leading. The words "received," "handed," and even "betrayed" all share the same connotation. Something is being handed over or passed between people. Communion fundamentally is an act that finds its action in face-to-face, intimate connection. Something odd happens when most Christians go to worship. For starters, most Christians don't share communion very often. And second, when we do, we take it in a way that we don't actually receive anything nor engage anyone. But I didn't have that option the Sunday I returned to the church that had given me my pink slip.

By the time of our visit, an occasional practice, sharing the Eucharist via intinction, had become the weekly practice. Intinction meant I had to walk down to the front of the auditorium, gather in a single-file line and be handed (receive) the bread from a server. At the moment of reception the words, "The body of Christ, broken for you," are pronounced by the server to the served. Next, you take your bread to another server holding the cup. You simply dip your bread into the wine as they say, "The blood of Christ shed for you." Just hearing words of forgiveness spoken over you grounds communion in much different soil than silently attempting to focus on Jesus as the plates bang and clash. But this Sunday there was more. As our family trekked forward to receive the Eucharist, my heart sank. More than that, my gut ached. I'd shown up that Sunday in some kind of attempt to come to terms with my own anger and hurt from the previous years, but I actually wanted mending to come when I wanted and as I wanted. I wanted to show them I was okay, had overcome, and was the bigger person because of my ability, like Muhammad Ali fighting George Foreman, to take their punches and emerge standing. But that went away when I realized my line for communion was being served by the church leader I thought most responsible for my dismissal. That's when the words, "You have to be $^$*%^*^* kidding me," leapt in my heart. I don't typically speak that way, but it came up and I couldn't stop it from coming. This, I was certain, was going to be the worst communion experience ever.

And that's when I remembered Paul and the Words of Institution. I was not taking something. I was *receiving* something. And that should make a difference. Like a birthday or Christmas gift, what I was being handed was for me, but not because of me. I was in the line of something that had long been in motion, and my only job was to take it and use it as intended.

My calluses became more tender.

When it was my turn, I walked to the front, opened my hands, and resolved to receive whatever I received as a gift. If some part of my mind and heart resisted, I would accept that I wasn't quite prepared to forgive as I should. If my mind and heart were opened to the point of tears, I would receive that as well. Much like rubbing alcohol to a wound, there was stinging and healing all at once. He smiled, stretched out his hand, looked me in the eyes, and said, "The body of Christ broken for you." I received it and I was changed. God performed a magnificent miracle, beyond my ability to control or understand. My openness to God created the space for my heart to open to others, to him. The events of our past did not disappear, but my hurt and anger, perhaps even my arrogance and pride, receded. Healing began. Reconciliation was birthed.

Healing and reconciliation is what it means to be church, to share communion. Healing and reconciliation is what Jesus intended our gatherings to be and to produce. I can't be reconciled alone. I can worship alone, but I can't commune alone. And I can't be reconciled with people who are already just like me. Church is more than a gathering of my friends, and communion demonstrates that. The differences, the tensions, the partisanship, the space between us create the opportunity for God to transform hearts from what they are not to what God created them to be.

If I believed communion was a snack for the baptized, a motivational tool for baptism or a time to sit in silence with my own thoughts, I could have communion anywhere. I can't. When Jesus gathers his first disciples at Passover and institutes communion, the cast of characters are men in desperate need of healing. There's Peter, whose only consistent virtue is his conflicting actions. One moment he trusts Jesus, in the next, not so much. Jesus knows Peter's denial is coming, but Peter shares communion with

Jesus. More scandalous is the presence of Judas, the betrayer. It's not shocking that Judas has dinner with Jesus, but that Jesus calls Judas out as the betrayer to his face, yet still eats with him and washes his feet.

As a youth worker, one my students worshipped with his girlfriend's church. When the time for the consecration of the elements came, the priest made it clear that for anyone present who was not a member of their denomination, the communion was closed and they could make their way to a special location in the sanctuary to receive a blessing. In the same way the church of my youth built fences around communion, this priest fails to realize what Jesus is doing with Peter and Judas. Communion itself is healing. Communion is the special place. That's what makes communion a special thing. One of the great heresies of the church is that our daily and weekly acts of love, service, and particularly worship are devoid of inherent and powerful significance on their own. How else can we explain the often flippant and mindless way we approach communion? Far too frequently we think of the elements of worship like children think of making their beds, "Why do it if we're just going to get back in it tonight and mess it up again?" as if there is no latent, deeply rooted, and lasting effect from the action. So, we try to insert random meaning to paper over the genetic force already at work if we choose to embrace it.

When my daughter asked, "Why are they mocking the poor?" she was reading 1 Corinthians with Paul's intention in full view. The Eucharist is thwarted—performed in an unworthy manner—whenever it is taken without regard for the healing and needs of the community. Paul scolds them:

> On this next matter, I wish I could applaud you; but I can't because your gatherings have become counterproductive, making things worse for the community rather than better. Let me start with this: I hear that your gatherings are polarizing the community; and to be honest, this doesn't surprise me. I've accepted the fact that factions are sometimes useful and even necessary so that those who are authentic and those who are counterfeit may be recognized. This distinction is obvious when you come together because it is not the Lord's Supper you are eating at all. When it's time to eat, some hastily dig right in; but look—some have more than others: over there someone is hungry, and over here someone is drunk! What is going on? If a self-centered meal is what you want, can't you eat and drink at home? Do you have so little respect for God's people and this community that you shame the poor at the Lord's table? I don't even know what to say to you! Are you looking for my approval? You won't find it. (1 Cor 11:17–22 The Voice)

In Corinth, the rich were gathering, eating communion, which at that time was served in the context of a meal, and mocking the poor by reminding them they were poor. By the time poor Christians showed up, not only had the rich had their fill, they had more than enough. They were drunk. They took communion like most of us do everything, with only their bellies, their immediate needs and desires, in sight. And when any act, religious or not, is performed with a concern for self over the concern for others, the inevitable result is polarization. A self-centered meal produces self-centered people. The people in Corinth, like people throughout all time, had a sense of status, and the Corinthians were preserving this status in how they ate and who they ate with. It's a problem that hasn't gone away.

Yet Jesus's table habits fight back against our tendency to sit and eat with people who are most like us. Not only that, Jesus's meals are more than symbols, and much more than a means by which to anger the Pharisees. There is one thing in common in all of Jesus's meals; there is an extension of grace in each. You cannot have a meal with Jesus present and not be offered grace, joy, and forgiveness. It happens at Simon's house (Luke 7:36–50), at Zaccheus' home (Luke 19:1–10), dining with Mary and Martha (Luke 10:38–42), and Passover. When Jesus, on the night he was betrayed, took bread and broke it and took wine and poured it, he was formalizing what he had done informally so many times before. The previous dinners were foreshadowing his last meal with his disciples. Jesus extends healing to Peter and Judas, perhaps, not because that's what he was feeling in the moment, but because that's what the meal does all on its own.

Eating together can be grace or anti-grace. We get to choose. What if at the heart of the Lord's Supper is not psychoanalytic and neurotic navel-gazing at our own sin, but mindful, compassionate consideration of those in our body, particularly those shamed by our world? This is what Paul means when he says, "Examine yourselves first. Then you can properly approach the table to eat the bread and drink from the cup" (1 Cor 11:28 NRSV). He is asking Christians to clear our hearts of worldly metrics that divide us into rich and poor, educated and uneducated, and even religious metrics like sinners and saints. And this can be done with a meal.

The Pharisees, like many of us today, ate in ways designed to polarize, to restate and entrench in the body what they already felt in their hearts. While eating together should birth unity, the Pharisees in the Corinthian church brought shame on the poor. This is where Paul's repeated arguments that humans are justified by faith matters in ways we often fail to acknowledge. While justification by faith typically serves to free us from the slavery of working for our personal salvation, it also has a leveling effect. If all those seated around the Lord's table are justified by faith, then what is most important about us and core to our identity—that we are "in Christ"—is unifying rather than divisive. So those in Corinth retaining a view of the world that is group based—financial, racial, religious, moral—are not only sinning and shaming, they are working against the grain and purposes of the cross. As Richard Rohr has said, "Everyone is in heaven when he or she has plenty of room for communion and no need for exclusion."[1] Paul argues, "When we give thanks and share the cup of blessing, are we not sharing in the blood of the Anointed One? When we give thanks and break bread, are we not sharing in His body? Because there is one bread, we, though many, are also one body since we all share one bread" (1 Cor 10:16–17 The Voice). The Lord's Supper offers believers a return to relationality that is obliterated when Christians exist in isolation and division. To share communion without a focus on the relational healing for which it, at least in part, exists, is to turn our backs on God's healing intent. Simply put: communion without communing is sinful. Consider also Paul's admonition to the church in Ephesus that "effectively the cross becomes God's means to kill off the hostility once and for all so that He is able to reconcile them both to God in this one new body" (Eph 2:16 The Voice).

One bread. One body.

Oneness, which requires relational healing, is the foundation of the Lord's table. We cannot have one without the other without eating and drinking judgment against ourselves. Paul tells the church to wait for one another to eat, but there's more to it than that. If some are hungry or poor, how could anyone possibly indulge or overeat? To wait for one another is to consider the needs, the lives, the hurts, pains, and joys of one another.

What is now undeniable is that Christian witness and hospitality are not and cannot be measured by how welcoming our churches feel to guests who drop in on Sunday. Extensions of grace occur at table, when spiritually formed women and men discern the others who join them at table. Who we eat with and what we do while there are far better indicators of whether or not we've become students of Jesus than almost anything we do. Yet, there is no Christian conference or leadership curriculum I'm aware of pinpointing the churches' near total abstention from broadening the Lord's table. In

1. Rohr, *Falling Upward*, 101.

fact, the Homogenous Unit Principle not only ignores the Lord's Supper, it gives us cotton candy and calls it a meal! In a world overflowing with group hostility, where harnessing the relational healing inherent in communion offers to make the world a more loving, hospitable, and gracious place, the church has decided to surrender avenues of healing in exchange for another moment for hastily served, breezy, personal musings. If the relational healing extended at Lord's Supper will be recovered in the church, it will first be recovered at dining tables, school cafeterias, and lunch groups.

In 2014 America was forced yet again to face the underlying racial and ethnic tensions that have always been at the root of our country. A grassroots movement, Black Lives Matter, emerged in response to the high-profile killings of unarmed black men by law enforcement such as Michael Brown, Eric Garner, Dontre Hamilton, John Crawford III, Ezell Ford, and others. In typical anti-communion fashion, American Christians and Americans in general ran to quarters and defended the actions of the groups and institutions they were previously aligned with. Scenes of destruction monopolized network and cable news night after night as places like Ferguson were alight with tension, tear gas, and law enforcement agencies armed to the teeth in the wake of the killing of Michael Brown. Ferguson looked like a war zone. I was particularly interested in Ferguson because I had spoken near there the previous summer in one of the most racially diverse churches I'd ever seen. But that Ferguson was in the rearview mirror. What fascinated me most was the way everybody just ran to their side, and few people were interested in what the story looked like from the other side. Whenever something like this happens, everyone just draws really predictable lines and demonstrates our unwillingness to discern our body politic.

I, too, am part of the problem. As I read the daily headlines I feel a surge of injustice in some of these cases. I was and am right for feeling that way. Like everyone, I have a battery of experiences and my own history that places me on one side of the debate more easily that the other side. I'm more sympathetic to one side than the other. You are, too, I'd bet. I was more than sympathetic. I was angry. Resentful. Mad. Scared. Worried for the world of my daughters.

Thanksgiving changed that.

That fall our family went to Houston to join my wife's family for Thanksgiving dinner. Rochelle is white; so are most of her family members. One of Rochelle's cousins, Andy, is a police office in Houston. I've known

Andy since he was fifteen and he has always been a good kid. After more fits than starts in his educational journey, Andy finally settled into the Police Academy and graduated. That Thanksgiving, Andy was headed to work right after we ate, so he showed-up in uniform with his side arm, Taser, and mace. He struggled to eat wearing his bulletproof vest, which looked more uncomfortable than a size twelve foot wedged into a size nine shoe. He wasn't the only one there who was uncomfortable. This was Thanksgiving. This was about family and table, but seeing Andy, armed and in uniform, recirculated every negative feeling and event about the handful of harsh and unqualified police men and women I'd ever encountered in my life. And the last thing I wanted anyone to say was anything that had to do with the headlines or the parade of dead unarmed black men littered across America.

Andy's wife, Heather, was there too, with their three children. After hurriedly eating, Andy got up, washed his hands, and headed to the door to start his shift on patrol. At the door Andy did what millions of husbands do every day when they go to work. He said goodbye. He kissed his wife.

I thought: they do this every day. And every day they do this, she doesn't know if he's coming home. Now, every day people leave home and don't make it back, and police officers being killed in the line of duty is relatively rare, about twenty-seven per year from nonaccidental gunfire, but the image is seared into my mind. When Heather says, "Be safe. I love you," there is a weight that doesn't exist when Rochelle says it to me.

Now that doesn't change anything! It doesn't change any opinions, perceptions, or thoughts, but, in the words of Paul, it is an opportunity to "examine yourself" and "wait for each other." It is a moment born from a meal together. At table we have one decision to make. We can choose to mock or choose to heal the distance between us. We can drink grape juice or real wine.

13

Welcoming Phoebe

Our heart is wide enough to embrace the world and hands
are long enough to encompass the world.

—Amit Ray, *Nonviolence: The Transforming Power*

I WAS SHOCKED AND MORE than a little saddened several Christmases ago
when multiple people I knew, all pastors, were fired from their churches
either right before or in the middle of the holidays. For whatever reason, a
few churches thought that Christmas was the best time to abandon ministers and their families with no income. As someone who has been termi-
nated from a ministry position, I know the sting and heartache. Pastors are
rarely told the truth about their dismissal and it almost always comes as
a blindside. Worse, in the times when others would turn to their pastors,
small group, or community of faith for succor, the fired pastor loses most
of her or his support system when they get their pink slip. Ministry is not
like other jobs. Churches, unlike schools or businesses or hospitals, aren't
ubiquitous. When you lose your job at your church that likely means moving to another city, maybe another state. Your spouse and kids all have to
uproot. When pastors lose their jobs, the loss is almost total. It's no wonder
to me that when some pastors get fired they decide to rarely, if ever, darken
the door of a church again.

During the blood-letting a few years ago, when minister after minister
I was acquainted with were being shown the door during Advent, another
friend, drawing from his own experience, offered a word of encouragement on Facebook. He wrote, "It's now been six months since my termina-
tion. It's also been six months since I last attended a worship service, class,

meeting, etc . . . . I've learned a few things from my sabbatical, but the most frightening is how incredibly irrelevant church is to people outside the church. The absence of church participation has ZERO functional impact on my day-to-day life." Do you ever feel like that? If you're reading this, you've got more than a passing interest in God and the church of Jesus, but have you ever felt like all of this "church" business, when you boil it all down, has zero impact? Maybe you've felt that church is even a hindrance to God? You're not alone if you do. People don't usually admit that church feels like it's having "zero impact" until they are on their way out or they've been hurt by church. And I don't think most of us find it incomprehensible when someone who has been abused by a church or someone who has only seen Christians and churches divide and bruise people says, "burn it down," like Jello Biafra said.

One of the books that saved my faith after I had been fired from a ministry position was Philip Yancey's *Soul Survivor: How My Faith Survived the Church*. Yancey profiles thirteen Christian women and men from recent history, telling their stories and how they navigated faith during difficult times while exemplifying the virtues of Jesus. I was at a crossroads. I wasn't in danger of losing my faith in God. I had lost my faith in people. Don't get me wrong. Not many people would have described me as a great believer in people to begin with. Like most of us, I've been disappointed and hurt enough for a lifetime. I wasn't naïve about what people are like. Unlike healthier people, too often I allow my hurt and disappointment to calcify into long-held resentments and visions of revenge. When I got fired my faith in God was sturdy. I'd lost faith in the church. The church, the body in which I'd loved and served my entire lifetime, turned on me and began shredding my insides like the brain of a patient dying of multiple sclerosis. Yancey was there for me. I was hooked from the first paragraph: "Sometimes in a waiting room or on an airplane I strike up a conversation with strangers, during the course of which they learn that I write books on spiritual themes. Eyebrows arch, barriers spring up, and often I hear yet another horror story about church. My seatmates must expect me to defend the church, because they always act surprised when I respond, 'Oh, it's even worse than that. Let me tell you my story.' I have spent most of my life in recovery from the church."[1]

Yancey, like me, had grown up in Georgia. The churches of his youth were harsh, abusive, and racist. Though decades older than me, Yancey's

1. Yancey, *Soul Survivor*, 1.

church experience wasn't incomprehensible to my own. The same was true of Martin Luther King Jr., Annie Dillard, and the other eleven faithful believers Yancey chronicled. Each story was simultaneously relatable and distant. I discovered that no one makes it through human interactions, even in the church of Jesus, without getting some of other people's mess on them. That's part of what we do together. The sticky, ugly smelliness of living in communion is not an unfortunate side effect of church life—it's the essence of it. *Soul Survivor* said it was about holding onto faith, but it opened a window to what a real church is—a diverse, all-inclusive body of believers who struggle together to walk with God. The thirteen women and men were not merely people of faith, like individually wrapped sticks of gum jammed into one package, but a quilt that required each one of them to shine in its own way in order to stay woven together. Yes, some of the edges frayed. There were holes in some patches, for sure, but that's what happens when a quilt is taken off the hanging rod and used in real life.

Like Yancey, I've met my share of the walking church wounded on airplanes. I used to lie when people asked me what I did for a living. I'd say anything besides "pastor," until God began steering me to people on planes who needed a pastor. My wife finds it startling and curious that on multiple occasions I've found myself on airplanes seated next to "dancers," and not dancers of the Alvin Ailey variety. These women danced around poles and were paid in one-dollar bills. And when I meet them, they always want to talk, maybe confess, about their current lives. Eventually I learned to stop lying and be available for God's purposes. I'm an introvert so I'm not typically interested in being trapped for hours talking to a complete stranger, but that's what kept happening. As a spiritual discipline of hospitality and openness to God and neighbor, I committed myself to asking my airplane seat mates, "Are you coming or going?" and allow God to use that question however God sees fit. But that's all I'm ever going to volunteer.

In 2015 I was flying home to Texas from Los Angeles. I'd been in California speaking and teaching for a week and was completely exhausted. It was the Friday red-eye. Early Saturday morning I was scheduled to run a 5K with my family and because I overestimated the amount of free time I would have in California, I had yet to complete Sunday's sermon. This flight, if I used my time wisely, would allow me to finish the sermon and get a quick snooze before landing in Austin. That didn't happen. I should've known I was in trouble when I sat down and saw that the guy next to me didn't have a book or a laptop. Beware seatmates who don't have a book or laptop. They think you're their entertainment. My seatmate started talking before the in-flight safety instructions. He was terribly interested in the fitness tracker I was wearing, and as he saw me open my iPad and begin typing notes for my sermon, the conversation suddenly took on a spiritual nature. First, he asked what I thought about the age of the earth. He then moved on to evolution and asked what I thought about the Bible and inspiration. He was well versed too. He knew more Bible than most of the people I meet on airplanes. His name was Troy and he is a physician. Fresh out of medical school, Troy was heading to Texas for his first job. In route, I guess he decided to burden me with a lifetime of his theological questions. After about an hour, we got to his real question. He wanted to ask me about his brother. Troy is a ginger-headed white guy from the Midwest. His brother is adopted and African-American. Troy wanted me to see his brother's wedding photos. His brother is gay. I'm sure Troy has legitimate questions about the age of the universe and evolution, but that's not what he really wanted from me. His real question was about how the church (Christians) viewed his brother and why we might view him that way. I'm sure there are exceptions, and notable ones, but in my experience when we dig into people's theological and philosophical questions, they are rarely all that theological or philosophical. They are almost always about people and how people are treated. Part of what makes us human is an inherent concern for the other humans we love. Troy wanted to know if Christians would love his brother the way he loved his brother and what we meant by love.

What I found interesting about Troy was his asking a complete stranger whether or not the church was welcoming or not. His brother lives in Pennsylvania. There's extraordinarily little chance either of them will darken the door of a church in Texas, but for whatever reason, Troy wanted to discover what Christians would do with people like him and his brother. I told Troy what I tell everyone, "Of course you and your brother would be welcomed at my church." This is, in my view, the easiest question in the world to answer. Maybe I should know more about the sexual habits of my church members, but I'm not worried about that any more than I'm worried about the hundred other sins present each Sunday in our pews. Our gatherings are predicated on the fact that we're sinners. We wouldn't gather otherwise.

My entire life Sunday morning worship gatherings have been chock full of sinful and struggling people. I've known wives who have been or are being abused by their husbands and our church leaders are active and involved in either healing or seeking immediate safety for them, whichever one is required. I also know that men and boys, one in three, I've heard, are locked into a death match with pornography. Some congregants arrive at worship having won a few rounds that week, others show up having lost every round all week. Years of ministry have brought me face-to-face with tax cheats, ex-cons, illegal immigrants, employers of illegal immigrants, adulterous spouses, drug users, sexually deviant couples, and every other lifestyle option Satan has encouraged believers to grasp hold of. On Sunday morning—not to mention weekly Bible classes, small groups, and women's and men's events—my church, and yours, is filled to overflowing with sinful people. Some of them just hide it better than others. Instead of being the place people recover from, the church should be the place where people recover.

For that to happen, all people have to be accepted in every church all the time. As Bob Goff says, "love everyone, always."

As we've explored, the New Testament church is not exclusive or obsessed with works of righteousness or self-concern. The Scriptures don't present a church consumed with its own preservation or the preservation of a culture or a nation. We see a church called to be gracious and open; embracing and hospitable, and most of all, peaceable. Paul spent his entire ministry career hashing out one central problem, the tension between Jews and Gentiles. These two groups learning to love and accept each other is the presenting problem, but the ultimate aim is to learn to love and welcome all people. The suspicion, distrust, issues surrounding works of the Torah, and religious superiority formed an impenetrable wedge between people. Paul's instruction to alleviate the distance? Get over yourself. Accept each other as Christ has accepted you so that you can get on with the ministry of reconciliation.

Paul makes this clear in 2 Corinthians 5:

> From now on, therefore, we regard no one from a human point of view; even though we once knew Christ from a human point of view, we know him no longer in that way. So if anyone is in Christ, there is a new creation: everything old has passed away; see, everything has become new! All this is from God, who reconciled us to himself through Christ, and has given us the ministry of reconciliation; that is, in Christ God was reconciling the world to himself, not counting their trespasses against them, and entrusting the message of reconciliation to us. So we are ambassadors for Christ, since God is making his appeal through us; we entreat you

> on behalf of Christ, be reconciled to God. For our sake he made
> him to be sin who knew no sin, so that in him we might become
> the righteousness of God. (2 Cor 5:16–21 NRSV)

What does this have to do with church and Troy's brother? Christian community is not about surrounding yourself with folks who think like, act like, dress like, worship, and sin like you. At the heart of community is reconciliation to God and the Other. This not only heals the human tensions but also allows believers to join God in God's mission to reconcile the world (2 Cor 5:16–21; Gal 3:15–29; Eph 2:11–22; Rom 12). The way Paul sees it, if your body lacks inclusive diversity and lacks meaningful engagement with God's mission, you have something, but it may not be a church. You can have a group, you can have a club, you can have people over for dinner, and sit in your living room or stand in an auditorium singing, but that's not what makes a church a church. You can also have support and fellowship but that doesn't make what you have a church either. Plenty of people claiming no kinship with Christ do those things all the time. They don't call it church, because the church is animated through reconciliation empowered by the Holy Spirit.

My liberal and progressive friends are very open to the idea of a church that embraces the Other. They would fawn over Troy's brother and pat themselves on the back for doing so. The Other is beloved in progressive communities as long as that Other is oppressed, poor, marginalized, a minority, a refugee, or disenfranchised. The Other who is a conservative, a complementarian, a neo-Calvinist, a Republican, guns in the basement homeschooler, or adherent to Quiverfull, or just an all-out jerk, is more readily seen as the opposition than the Other. Paul seems to think that being in the presence of the Other—even the "annoying, conservative Other"—is what it means to be church. We can't quit each other.

And the church is more than a collection of friends, as well. It's becoming more and more popular to look around the table at our friends and call those people "our community" that we "do life together" with, but that is a miserly view of community that frees us from having to grow or develop. If we are not intentionally around people who are different from us, we have formed a clubhouse and not much more. Could it be that our friends only have so much to teach us and there is greater growth available in listening to and being challenged by those who try and test us? What about those who are actively working for a different kind of politics and policy than ours? What about those whose sins we find repugnant or don't understand? God finds all our sins repugnant. This is one of the reasons we need church, to encourage us to be around people we wouldn't choose, so we can become the kinds of people who love God and love neighbor regardless of who the neighbor is.

Both progressives and conservatives easily opt for their worldview instead of their brothers and sisters. By doing so they both choose their vision of what church life should be and neglect the ministry of reconciliation. Both sides miss the idea that involvement in the ministry of reconciliation means engaging people with whom we have real and considerable differences.

For progressives, when the frailty of their psyches meets the Other who is unlike them or disagrees with them, they check out and leave church altogether. Though many who leave church out of frustration or what they deem to be theological narrowness bristle at being labeled selfish participants in consumer Christianity, I cannot imagine how anyone can perform the ministry of reconciliation in the world if they cannot do so in the same pew. As a matter of fact, if we cannot reconcile inside communities of faith, we cannot reconcile at all. There is no such thing as selective reconciliation!

At the same time, many of my conservative friends constantly urge people to remain in church—if they will restrict their sins to the pre-approved ones—remain quiet, and just accept the long-established teaching of the church. They're banking on loyalty. Loyalty demands that the troubled and questioning "stay, stay, stay, unless you have some exceptionally good reason to leave." But Christian community is broader and more meaningful than staying for the sake of staying or leaving just because someone gets on your theological nerves.

I was raised in churches that grew and maintained themselves through the inertia of brand loyalty. As more people came to different conclusions regarding privileged texts, my movement has receded. Loyalty, for most, is a poor long-term motivator. Paul knew this. For that reason, Christian community has never been built around loyalty, but the ministry of reconciliation. Pharisees were loyal, but that's partly why they missed God's mission and couldn't see God's love for the irreligious and disloyal. My conservative friends have something besides a church, too, when they expect fidelity to the old ways—a Bible study club or mutual edification society perhaps. We cannot fool ourselves into the misguided belief that because most congregants agree with the contents, lifestyles, and speech of a local body that that means they are a church. Loyalty does not create a church and those banking on allegiance should not be surprised if those interested in God's mission pack up and head out. If a church is not focused in God's reconciliation project it may not be a church.

Reconciliation is the only glue strong enough to bond all the differences inherent to humankind while also being seductive enough to invite others into it. Churches are all-inclusive, diverse bodies who deliberately join God's ministry of reconciliation. That means the place for Troy's brother is not just my church, but every church. It is the same hope for all those who were once—or who are currently—far from God. How else can any of us hope to encounter God and be transformed by God's spirit among God's people if God's people refuse our presence among them?

In Romans, Paul makes this subversive argument through the life of a woman named Phoebe.

> I commend to you our beloved sister Phoebe; she serves the church in Cenchrea as a faithful deacon. It is important that you welcome her in the Lord in a manner befitting your saintly status. Join in her work, and assist her in any way she needs you. She has spent her energy and resources helping others, and I am blessed to have her as my benefactor as well. (Rom 16:1–2 The Voice)

Twenty years ago in my tribe, the most scrutinized portion of Paul's concluding words would have been Paul's reference to Phoebe as a "deacon." Deacon was a role we believed was available only to men. And believe it or not, many people were shocked to discover the word "deacon" and a woman's name in the same sentence. We were either completely ignorant or tried to be.

The Romans didn't share our ignorance. They knew deacon meant "servant." They also knew that deacons were leaders in the church. Paul knows that they know. The Roman churches didn't need instruction about what the word meant. What they had to be told was how to *treat* a woman deacon.

If we hopped into the DeLorean, flipped on our Flux Capacitor, and traveled back in time, we'd better understand how vital this is. Women had little to no status in the ancient world. With a few rare exceptions, a woman could not rise above being property of either her father or her husband. Paul writes to a world that wouldn't merely anticipate a woman leader, but would find it utterly disquieting. And in a world of few hotels and vandals around every corner, travelers, as Pheobe would have been, were dependent on the hospitality of strangers. A priest and rabbi ignoring a beaten man on the side of the street, a knock at midnight unanswered, and angels awaiting hospitality in Sodom and Gomorrah are more than children's stories. They speak to the responsibility of God's people to welcome and accept strangers. Those who do not extend hospitality are not guilty of unneighborliness as much as they are guilty of sin.

Paul says to "welcome" Phoebe partly because Phoebe is the one who is carrying the letter. She's the delivery woman. This letter about how God is justified in loving and accepting whoever God chooses to love, this letter about how God has elected to save everyone who chooses him, this letter calling people of difference to love and accept each other is hand delivered by someone both Jews and Gentiles would be resistant to accept; a woman leader. Neither in first-century Palestine nor first-century Rome was there much idea about how to treat a woman in formal leadership over men. Paul says, "welcome" Phoebe.

Those who know Paul's letters understand the letter carrier often has much to do with the letter. Why is Paul so explicit that they treat her in accordance with her status? Why wouldn't they know instinctively to trust and follow her? This community called "church" is unlike anything in the world, which means the church must reject common views of seeing people for the way things actually are. The rules the world plays by are not the rules the church plays by. In the world, if you're rich, if you're wealthy, good-looking, skilled, gifted, from a good family, or well educated it matters in how people are received. Race, gender, sexuality, class, and economics: In the church, none of that matters. And that's not just true of Phoebe.

Last year I spoke for a mega church in southern California with over ten services each weekend. As much of a grind as preaching ten times a weekend is for a pastor, it must be even worse for the multiple people who work behind the scenes to create worship and holy spaces for thousands of people, especially the band. As I sat next to the church's senior pastor he whispered to me, "I wish everyone knew the stories of the people on that stage." He told me about their pianist, a man in his late fifties banging out a Hillsong United anthem, but had come to their church after thirty years of playing the organ at a dying Baptist church a few miles away. He found in this church an excitement and vitality that had escaped him all his life. The pastor went down the line telling me about the lead singer, a muscle-bound boxer, weight lifter, and former drug dealer whose gentle spirit was helping heal a crime-riddled community in the city. Story after story of people being used by God, both in worship services on the weekends and in their work lives every week. Powerful stories. These are the stories churches are eager to hear. Stories of changed lives who are changing lives. Then he told me what came to be my favorite story. It was a story about an unchanged life.

The young woman playing drums that night had been worshipping with their church for just under a year. She was in her late twenties and broke most stereotypes of young women. She was squat with short, unkempt hair and wearing cargo shorts and flannel shirt. The pastor explained to me that after a few weeks playing in the worship band she approached one of their worship leaders with a confession and a question. She had been raised in church and her parents had always been faithful, but since her earliest memories she sensed she didn't fit in with the rest of the girls and ever since she was a teenager she questioned her sexuality. What she wasn't certain of was what her lesbianism meant for her relationship with God. The worship leader brought the question to the senior pastor. The three of them talked and prayed about her place in the church and her relationship with God. In the end, they decided to do what churches should do, the same thing Paul invited the Romans to do with Phoebe. They welcomed her. My friend, the senior pastor, told her, "We can't answer all the questions that you have. We don't know what you're dealing with, but as you work through your struggle, work through it here."

Work Through It Here

Jesus has a quirky little statement in Luke 19 that most modern Christians don't know what to do with. As he enters Jerusalem for Passover, the last week of his earthly life, the crowds cheer and praise him, but in their typical reactionary fashion, the religiously minded and puritanical Pharisees, urge Jesus to get his people under control. Why? Because the people rightly recognize and worship Jesus as king, saying, "Blessed is the king, who comes in the name of the Lord! Peace in heaven, and glory in the highest heaven!" (Luke 19:38b). Jesus then makes it clear that he believes about himself what the crowd's singing proclaims, that he is God and even created and lifeless things, such as rocks, will cry out in praise to him. Finally, the Lord responds, weeping over the city and saying, "If you, even you, had only recognized on this day the things that make for peace! But now they are hidden from your eyes" (Luke 19:41–42). In the Gospel of Luke, we never hear explicitly from the Pharisees again. They fade into distance like the lost horizon in the rearview mirror. The Pharisees and their way of sorting the world into categories of those made pure by their religious works and those made impure because of their failures to adhere to those same religious works is a world only growing dimmer. Jesus's life and investment is for those, like Peter and Judas who enter Jerusalem with him, who are willing to join the journey, not for those who have assumed they've arrived. As Fr. Richard Rohr has said, "Jesus is never upset with sinners; he is only upset with people who do not think they are sinners." The Pharisees had become so aghast at perceived threats to their undefiled religion that they failed to see the God opportunity in front of them, Jesus in their midst. The Pharisees had front row seats to the visitation of God, new wine in new wineskins, a fresh move of the Spirit, and rather than discerning whether God was birthing a new way of being in the world and a new way for God's people to relate to one another, they recoiled into the inadequate and enfeebled mechanisms of their fragmentary vision of God. That reaction, Jesus says, is contrary to what makes for peace. And might it be possible that our failures to welcome others are akin to the Pharisees' failure to recognize Jesus? Could we too, by creating church environments where rejection is a reflex, also miss a visitation by God?

Paul speaks much more explicitly about peace in Ephesians 2 when he describes Jesus as "our peace" who "has made both groups into one and has broken down the dividing wall, that is, the hostility between us" (Eph 2:14 NRSV). There is a correlation between the hostility we feel and our ability to receive Jesus as Lord. One of the dominant temptations in the church is to believe the totality of the body of Christ is limited to those most like us. The theologically liberal and conservative each find ways to claim the un-Christ-like-ness of the other. Obviously, in the course of life together there are times when it's important to rebuke and strengthen our brothers and sisters, but that's seldom what we do. What happens much more often is we dismiss them. While the Scriptures call us to welcome those we might not expect as emissaries for Jesus and ambassadors for the Kingdom, repudiation is a much more seductive feeling. When looking at the totality of Paul's letters, it is impossible to dismiss the preeminence of welcome in the Christian life. And right now, Christians may need to make welcome and hospitality the central behavior of our corporate life together.

If your home, heart, and church are anything like mine, there are some people who are welcomed, celebrated, and loved easily and there are others who are harder to take. Christians have even created churchy language to smooth over our inability to embrace. We call some people "extra grace people." There are no such people. There are some people we are open to and others we are not. It's our problem, not a grace problem. Grace can handle it. Phoebe can serve as a template for the way believers are to receive and embrace people who are outside of our existing categories of who is acceptable to God. Since earlier in Romans, Paul has leveled the playing field and demonstrated that the driving force of the gospel is grace, neither the sin-filled life of others nor the righteous life remain distinctions by which to spurn one another. To welcome others is to move the focus away from what we think and center the spotlight on what others need. That is why Paul tells the Roman church to "welcome her in the Lord as is fitting for the saints, and help her in whatever she may require from you" (Rom 16:2). Welcome is a discipline of self-denial. It is the abnegation of compelling in others what we want and how we think things ought to be in order to live in harmony with our brothers and sisters. Welcome does not require our agreement nor consent with other's lifestyle choices. It only requires our care. People like Troy are not interested in what the church condones if we have not first demonstrated our care, even in the face of lifestyles we may disagree with.[2] If we cannot welcome God's children and recognize the image of God in one another, we will continue to abuse one another in the name of God and under the banner of the church.

Because my wife serves on the board of a ministry designed to help churches, schools, and families have better conversations about LGBTQ issues, we hear our fair share of stories of the ways families and churches have both rejected and welcomed those within the LGBTQ community. I'll never forget Ray's story.

Ray was raised a church kid like me, a card-carrying Southern Baptist. Like my denomination, his did not have a long history of accepting outsiders, much less people living "alternative lifestyles." Ray is a few years older than I am and there were many fewer places to go and people to talk with about his sexuality when he was a teenager. What Ray did know was that he was gay. During high school and a little during college, Ray dated girls, hoping against hope that a switch would flip and he'd feel the same thing for girls that all the other boys did. It never happened.

After college, Ray became a Catholic priest. Because he'd always been a devout God-follower and thoughtful Bible student, the priesthood offered

2. My point here is not to litigate whether or not particular acts are sinful or acceptable. There is a time and place for that, but before accountability for any thought or behaviors can take place, welcome and hospitality are necessary to create space for people to share mutual edification and discipleship.

an obvious excuse for not dating and everything within him still longed for a touch of magic that would cure him of his same-sex attraction. It never did. Over the years, Ray kept his head down, performed his duties, and tried to hide the romantic reflexes that he felt had always been a part of him. Against all his planning, Ray fell in love with a man named Michael. He attempted to lay aside the relationship, but it kept boomeranging back to him. Ray and Michael met at church and what they felt for one another, as they describe it, was deep and immediate. It took years for anything to come of the relationship. Ray deferred and deflected as long as he could. Eventually he decided to pursue and enjoy a relationship with Michael. Michael was brought to him by God, Ray truly believed it. Michael was thoughtful, fun, and like Ray, endeavored to follow God to the best of his ability. As Ray made changes in his life, one of which was moving from the Catholic priesthood to the Episcopal priesthood, his mind never released his greatest and most secretive fear: telling his parents about Michael.

Through all of Ray's theological explorations and changes, his parents had always been supportive, but they didn't harbor the same questions about God and sexuality that Ray did. Ray's parents were still a part of the same church where Ray was born and raised. He didn't know how they were going to take the news. Part of him wished they would be adamantly opposed. If so, Ray could expose them to the blistering critiques of his childhood church. Seminary education had given him plenty of ammunition to go toe-to-toe against all things conservative. At the same time, he wanted what all children want, need, and expect from their parents; complete, total, and unconditional embrace.

Ray decided to break the news on his next visit home.

Like Esther, Ray thought he would drop the news at dinner on his first night home. There was no purpose in allowing the stress to linger and the anxiety was festering all through his body, but his courage failed him. On their second night together, as his parents were putting the final touches on the family dinner, Ray launched his long-rehearsed discourse.

"Mom, Dad, you're probably wondered why I'm leaving the priesthood."

"We thought about it."

"Well, it's because I've fallen in love."

"Really?" asked Ray's mom.

"Yes."

"Well," said Ray's mom, "I figured that was what happened. Being a Catholic priest can be a lonely life. I told you that."

"I know. You were right. But I don't think I'm going to be alone much longer. So . . . "

"Before you go on," interjected Ray's dad, "let me ask you one question."

"Okay."

"Is it a man?"

Ray was stunned to the point of confusion. Had he ever slipped? Did he say or do something as a boy that had given him away? Had a post on Facebook or some slip of the tongue exposed Ray as gay? If so, had that been why his parents had responded so favorably to his Catholicism? Were they embarrassed by him? Had they seen the priesthood as a ruse to avoid incessant questioning and an attempt to live for God and break free from feelings none of them wanted Ray to feel? A thousand unplanned inquiries scampered through Ray's mind. This was not how he envisioned this conversation. His father had stolen his thunder and Ray had no clue how it happened or what end it served.

"Um . . . well, Dad, it's a man. His name is Michael."

Ray's dad's mouth crawled upwards at the corners. A twinkle glinted in his eye. "When do we get to meet him?"

14

Long Lost Love

Okay. Okay. All right, then, we'll do it. Whatever it takes.

— Karin, *Lars and the Real Girl*

IN MAY 2012, MARINA Keegan graduated from Yale University. She graduated the way many parents want their children to graduate college, with a job. Marina was going to write for *The New Yorker*. Before graduating, Marina wrote an essay for her graduating class entitled "The Opposite of Loneliness." It was distributed during commencement, and this is part of what she wrote:

> We don't have a word for the opposite of loneliness, but if we did, I could say that's what I want in life. What I'm grateful and thankful to have found at Yale, and what I'm scared of losing when we wake up tomorrow and leave this place.
>
> It's not quite love and it's not quite community; it's just this feeling that there are people, an abundance of people, who are in this together. Who are on your team. When the check is paid and you stay at the table. When it's four a.m. and no one goes to bed. That night with the guitar. That night we can't remember. That time we did, we went, we saw, we laughed, we felt. The hats.
>
> Yale is full of tiny circles we pull around ourselves. A cappella groups, sports teams, houses, societies, clubs. These tiny groups that make us feel loved and safe and part of something even on our loneliest nights when we stumble home to our computers— partner-less, tired, awake. We won't have those next year. We won't live on the same block as all our friends. We won't have a bunch of group-texts.

This scares me. More than finding the right job or city or spouse—I'm scared of losing this web we're in. This elusive, indefinable, opposite of loneliness. This feeling I feel right now. . . .

We don't have a word for the opposite of loneliness, but if we did, I'd say that's how I feel at Yale. How I feel right now. Here. With all of you. In love, impressed, humbled, scared. And we don't have to lose that.

We're in this together, 2012. Let's make something happen to this world.[1]

What Marina writes about stirs deeply within me because it reflects much of what I experienced as a college student. I was in college before the age of group texts, but we managed to find a way to bind our lives together in such tightly-knit community that it seemed odd and anxiety producing when we realized we'd leave school and head in different directions to begin again. Maybe that "opposite of loneliness" time isn't college for everyone. Maybe it was high school or young adulthood. Perhaps it's when people strike out into the world for the first time. Many people grow up in small towns like I did. In those places, there are always other kids to go outside and play with. As a boy, there were always people around, always a community to belong to. Marina's college experience was so densely populated, it was the opposite of loneliness. Marina writes about a basic human need; a need shared among all populations throughout history, the need for community.

It's not accidental that the story of God is a story of community that begins in community. "Then God said, 'Let us make humankind in *our* image, according to *our* likeness'" (Gen 1:26a). God exists, not as one God in a temple somewhere standing above everything else, but as one God in three persons, living in community. Not only that, but throughout the Scriptures the Godhead (YHWH, Jesus, and the Holy Spirit) consistently redirect the attention to other members of the Trinity. The entirety of the Hebrew Scriptures point to Jesus. Jesus, in turn, promotes and promises the coming and power of the Holy Spirit, and the Holy Spirit, in part, turns believers' hearts back to God. God's community is revolving. But community doesn't stop there. When God first creates humankind, God creates Adam alone, and quickly realizes that Adam's isolation is not good. God creates Eve and gives them the command to be fruitful and multiply. As they do, more and more people populate the earth, until God, in Genesis 12, calls Abram to form a

1. Keegan, "Opposite of Loneliness."

special community by which God will save the world. As the story unfolds, this is precisely what occurs through the death, burial, and resurrection of Jesus. In the aftermath of Jesus's ascendency to the right hand of God, the Apostle Paul then invites the entire world—as we've discussed previously— to be a part of God's ever-increasing community. This community, centered around God, remains a community and is identified as God's family in the final revelation: "After this I looked, and there was a great multitude that no one could count, from every nation, from all tribes and peoples and languages, standing before the throne and before the Lamb, robed in white, with palm branches in their hands" (Rev 7:9 NRSV).

From beginning to end, the story of God and God's created beings is one of community, not individuals. Individually, though, is the way many Christians conceive of their faith, as if there is little to nothing about their faith that regards other people, including our fellow believers, as necessary. In America, where I am fortunate enough to have been born, we are incredibly blessed. But one of the ideas we've inherited through our national narrative is the notion that the individual is the center of society. The same narrative informs us that the best way to produce human flourishing is to strengthen the individual. Therefore, we've created a hyper focus on individual rights. The way forward in our world is to make the most of your individual abilities. Freedom is defined by our ability to individuate.

All of this may be a great way to run a government, but if the writers of the New Testament were plopped down in the middle of modern-day churches, they would not understand how we transitioned from the life of community to our current focus on individuals.

They would not understand that most of us only see each other one or two times a week. They would not understand that older women and widows were often lonely and younger moms with children often felt overwhelmed. They would not understand that men—at every age—feel largely friendless. They would not understand that some of us have great weekend getaways while others of us scrape by financially. They would not understand people having a physical or financial need and keeping it secret. These acts, I think, would absolutely be mind-boggling. The first Christians gathered nearly everyday, shared their possessions, and bore one another's burdens. What the Scriptures teach is that when you and I are buried with Christ in baptism, we are raised into a new family—family that is supposed to love and care for one another as dearly as we do for our earthly families. Those first believers were not perfect, but they were connected. That's why throughout the New

Testament, the apostles write using language like "brothers and sisters," or "dear children." The people of God are a very large family, with God as Father and Jesus as the older brother. It's also why overwhelmingly the Scriptures say "our father," and "our lord," and only a few times says, "my lord."

The church has always been about the community.

The Gospel According to Dagmar

One of the more unexpected places the Bible's vision of the church as community shows up is one of my favorite movies, *Lars and the Real Girl*. The movie was no box-office smash, but *Lars* is the most moving and appealing example of what it means to be a Christian community.

Ryan Gosling play Lars Lindstrom, a loveable but mentally disturbed twenty-seven-year-old man. Lars, as far as we can tell (and I'm leaning on my wife's training as a therapist), suffers from a dissociative disorder, resulting in the breakdown of his identity and perception. He lives in the garage behind the house where he grew up and where his brother, Gus, and sister-in-law, Karin, now live. Gus and Karin are expecting their first child, but as busy as they are, Karin makes it her goal to connect with Lars, but to no avail. Lars is isolated and does little more than attend church and go to work. At work Lars endures a porn-obsessed coworker, Kurt, and actively avoids Margo, who is secretly in love with him and desperately trying to get Lars to notice her. One day, Kurt tells Lars about customizable, anatomically correct sex dolls that can be ordered from the Internet. As disturbed and lonely as Lars is, he orders a doll. A few weeks later, Lars finally takes Karin up on her repeated offers to come over to the house for dinner. He asks if he can bring a guest, his new girlfriend, Bianca. Gus and Karin couldn't be more excited, thinking that Lars has made a real connection with someone, *finally*. They burst with excitement that Lars has anyone in his life. But when Lars appears at dinner, it's just Lars and his sex doll.

Bewildered doesn't even begin to describe Gus's and Karin's reaction to Bianca. They sit in the living room chatting and eat dinner, all with Lars behaving as if Bianca is 100 percent real. Lars gives Gus and Karin Bianca's entire life story. Lars explains that he and Bianca met on the Internet (which is true, technically), that she doesn't speak much English, is a missionary on sabbatical, and confined to a wheelchair, and that because she is religious, Lars requests that Bianca stay in the house rather than with him in the garage.

Gus is despondent. His little brother is insane and talking to a doll.

Trying to break Lars from his delusion, Gus and Karin convince Lars that since Bianca has just arrived from outside the country, a trip to the town doctor, Dagmar, who happens to be a family practice doctor and a psychiatrist, might be in order. Lars agrees.

That night in bed, Gus is disconsolate. "What will people think?" Gus asks Karin.

"We can't worry about that."

The next morning all four—Gus, Karin, Lars, and Bianca—make an appointment to see Dagmar. Dagmar takes Bianca's blood pressure and treats her like a real patient. She diagnoses Bianca with low-blood pressure and tells Lars she needs to see Bianca once a week for "treatment." In a private meeting with Gus and Karin, Dagmar tells them that she thinks Lars is trying to communicate or work something out. Bianca is in town for a reason and she's not going anywhere. Treat her as real, Dagmar urges them, because she is real to Lars.

"People will laugh at him," Gus shoots back to Dagmar.

"And they'll laugh at you too."

Gus and Karin are laughed at. Karin and her friends joke about how anatomically correct Bianca is. Gus's coworkers make Lars and Bianca the butt of their jokes. One of Gus's coworkers even says he envies Lars: "I wish I had a woman who couldn't talk." Yet all of that is prelude to the main event. What's going to happen when Lars and Bianca show up at church?

To prepare the way for Lars and Bianca, Gus and Karin meet with the Bible study class, which includes the church's pastor, Reverend Bock. Their opinions are all over the place. One man suggests Bianca is like a golden calf. Another chafes at the idea of a sex doll coming to church, even after it's made clear Lars is not having sex with Bianca. Mrs. Gruner, the prophet of Holy Grace Lutheran Church, ends the discussion.

"Sally, your cousin puts dresses on his cats. Hazel, your nephew gave all his money to a UFO club. Arnie, everyone knows your first wife was a klepto."

"She wasn't."

"Then how come she's buried in a pair of my earrings? . . . .These things happen. Lars is a good boy. You can depend on me."

And as the church goes, so does the town. The welcome Bianca receives from the church is the welcome she receives from everyone in town.

When Lars and Bianca show up at church, they garner their fair share of stares, but they are received with open arms and kind words.

As Lars and Bianca leave church that first Sunday, Mrs. Gruner hands Bianca the flowers from the church altar. Lars tells Bianca, "Isn't that great? They're not real so they'll last forever." At this point, we learn more about Lars. Like everyone else you've ever known, Lars's behavior makes sense in context. We learn that Gus left home while Lars was still young. At a young age, Lars was left with a drunken, bitter dad. Their mother died before Lars had any memory of her and he has never been able to connect intimately with anyone. Bianca's parents, like Lars's mother, died when she was young. It's an experience they share. Each treatment for Bianca is actually a therapy session for Lars. In one of their sessions we discover that physical contact with another person is physically painful. It burns. But it doesn't hurt Lars to touch Bianca.

As the story moves forward, the townspeople do for Bianca what the church did for Bianca. They accept her completely. Bianca is driven around town running errands. Karin's friends take her to get her hair done. Bianca gets a job as a model at a clothing store in the mall and is even elected to the school board. The town lavishes love upon Bianca. She becomes a conduit of love and acceptance to and from Lars. In the process Lars comes to understand how to be a real person.

It's crazy, right? Just the stuff of Hollywood? But it's so much more, because the town doesn't care about Bianca. They care about Lars. Having his time with Bianca whittled away by work, friends, and volunteering, Lars feels abandoned and frustrated. As his irritation mounts, Lars begins to argue with Bianca. One night Lars rants about feeling discarded by Bianca. He is livid that she keeps going on and is unsettled by the fact that no one cares.

Karin meets Lars in the backyard to set him straight about the reality of what is actually happening.

Lars grumbles, "Everyone just does what ever they want to."

Karin yells back Lars, "That is just not true! Every person in this town bends over backwards to make Bianca feel at home! Why do you think she has so many places to go and so much to do? Huh? Huh? . . . Because you, because all these people love you. We push her wheelchair, we drive her to work, we drive her home, we carry her, we get her up, we put her to bed, and she is not petite, Lars. Bianca is a big, big girl. None of this is easy for any of us, but we do it for *you*. So don't you dare tell me how we don't care."

It is all for Lars. When the community sees a need in their midst, their response is to surrender their entire being for the sake of the hurting. Bianca isn't real, but Lars is and Lars matters. Where the easiest thing to do with Lars is what Gus wanted to do, lock him away someplace, it would not be as healing as loving Lars through it. Judgment and cynicism, mockery and criticism, seem sophisticated, but anyone who's ever been on a kindergarten playground has plenty of evidence that it's not. Gus worries about looking stupid and being judged. Those same fears lived in the shallow bucket as my anxieties about extending kindness to Rat Girl in high school. There's nothing sophisticated about it. It's boring and jaded. Screenwriter Nancy Oliver says she asks herself, "If there are so many desperate people walking around . . . what would happen if we treated their illnesses and their delusions with compassion, acceptance and tolerance instead of this shunning thing we do?" I wonder that, too. And I wonder if the kind ones (*chrestos*) are the ones God expects to do it.

As more people reach out to Bianca, Lars's own reach expands. His connection to Margo grows deeper as he notices her noticeable longing for him. And as he does, Bianca becomes less significant. Soon, Bianca becomes ill. She is rushed to the hospital (remember this is a sex doll). Dagmar and Lars tell Karin and Gus that Bianca is very sick. In fact, she's dying. She's sick and won't recover. As the news reverberates across town Lars awakes the next morning surrounded by love. His front porch is covered with flowers, gift baskets, candles, and get-well balloons. There's also a bag of mail. The entire town is praying for Bianca. Later that evening, three women, Mrs. Gruner, Mrs. Petersen and Mrs. Schindler, all from church, invite Lars downstairs where they sit rocking and doing needlepoint.

Lars asks, "Is there something I should do?"

"No dear. You eat," responds Mrs. Gruner.

Mrs. Schindler placidly jumps in, "We came over to sit."

"That's what people do when tragedy strikes."

"They come over and sit."

I don't want to spoil the ending for you, but *Lars and the Real Girl* is the most beautiful meditation on Christian love put on film in my lifetime. It's not like most movies marketed to Christians, which are essentially ninety-minute sermons with poor production values, C-minus acting, and a heavy-handed script. Lars's story is about one man finding himself. You'll have to watch until the end to see how, but it is also about the church, a church living, working, and loving as a community of hospitality and acceptance.

The church plays a pivotal role in Lars's healing. When we first meet him, Lars is on his way to church. Four of the film's critical scenes occur with the church or in the worship of the church. Every major character in the movie worships at Holy Grace Lutheran Church, and they show the world what welcome, love, and hospitality really are. The church is the hub of the wheel for life and culture. This is a lesson for every Christian around the world who wants their culture to reflect Christian values. This is how God's kingdom blooms, through acceptance, hospitality, and the extension of grace. Three of the four church scenes in *Lars and the Real Girl* take place in worship. In all three scenes the sermons are about love. What is a church, if not a place where all people can love and be loved? Lars, just like everyone you've ever known, finds transformation and healing through the undeniable and breath-taking power of love. Ryan Gosling, who played Lars, said, "Lars doesn't make the choice to be loved, he makes the choice to love. It doesn't need to be a transaction. You can just give."

Everything the church attempts to do in the world should be summed up in our choice to love.

Inside the human heart lies a reflex to criticize, judge, distance, and segregate. Human history has already demonstrated that, but the church's job is to form a new reflex to love. If Jesus is doing anything through his words and actions, he is rearranging our instinct to choose judgment over love. James, the brother of Jesus, tells Christians to choose "mercy over judgment" as another way to refresh our eyes concerning the church's vocation. In Jesus's mind, judgment should be a chore and love should be a reflex. When Paul talks about what is most important he says, "But now faith, hope, and love remain; these three virtues must characterize our lives. The greatest of these is love" (1 Cor 13:13 The Voice). And this is how the world will know that we are his disciples.

Long Lost Love

In 2012 I attended a conference about "disciple making." I spent two days listening to and learning from speakers and teachers share about "making disciples." The opening speaker wanted to make one thing clear: The church is in trouble. According to a poll, some Christians didn't believe what he thought they ought to believe about baptism or hell or atonement theory. Even more Christians polled confessed to premarital sex and Christian divorce rates were inching up. He also said we should all be ashamed of not fully embracing the theology of adoption from Romans and adopt little black kids from Africa. If I didn't know before, I knew now: we pastors aren't "making disciples" (or at least that guy's version of one). I wanted to tell him, I've already got two little black kids.

The conference only got worse. Over the two days, speakers reinforced how we weren't "doing enough," or "teaching the gospel enough," or "serving the community enough." There were a lot of "enoughs."

We also heard about what a waste of time it was to "preach sermons" and how "people aren't interested in your ivory tower theology." All of this, of course, was done in the service of getting us pastors to "make disciples." I discovered we weren't doing enough, because I wrote it all down in my "you suck at ministry" notebook they placed in our goody bags. But there was a huge gap in my notes. Not a single speaker mentioned love or how to better love those in our communities who were in some way like Lars— marginalized, suffering, disengaged, lonely, and lost. Even the portions of the content that were geared toward being "missional" spun the meaning of "missional" into a weave of complex manipulations to get our neighbors to become members of our churches through various kind of charity. Charity is good. It's a form of love, it's the manipulations that are the problem. If love is not self-seeking, neither should expressions of love distributed by the church be self-seeking. Many contemporary churches are experiencing a long lost love. Under the rubble of our concerns about politics, a changing culture, the decline in religious participation, and sexuality, we have lost the ability, and maybe even the desire, to simply love people.

This, too, is part of the story we have lost.

Turns out, Christians will not be known as Jesus's disciples by the votes we cast or our positions on policy. We won't be known by our church doctrines, it's size, or whether we "leveraged our leadership." We won't even be known by moral accomplishments. Jesus says that we will be known by our love!

Before we can do anything and call it Christian, we are asked to love. Those who follow Jesus are expected to love first—without hesitation, without pre-condition, without any "Yeah, I know, but what about people who (insert your favorite issue here)." When Jesus is asked what is the greatest command, he responds, "Love God and love your neighbor."

But Christians don't always act that way. Christians often act like the greatest command is to tell everyone what all the other commands are. We cannot be the people of God much less invite others into the reign of God by ignoring the first rule of God: love.

We are to love everybody. No exceptions!

Jesus is not naïve or stupid. He knows terrorists exist. He knows people engage in sexually unorthodox behaviors (both Christians and non-Christians). God knows humans disagree about God's existence. Jesus knows there are Democrats and Republicans who are sharply divided about nearly everything. He knows some people are pro-Israel, anti-Israel, or don't care about Israel. Jesus knows some people pay more taxes while others pay less. Jesus knows there are racists and sexists and bigots and backstabbers. Jesus knows each of us will have some person or group we don't like, but he gives us no caveat: "Love your enemies and pray for those who persecute you" (Matt 5:44).

We are free to hold convictions about multiple social, national, and international issues and conflicts. We are free—even encouraged, when appropriate—to work for political and social justice. We are not free, however to hold those convictions, regardless of what they are, in the absence of love. Jesus knows what history should have taught us: conviction without love ends in oppression.

Lars brings a sex doll to dinner. Gus and Karin have no clue what to do. Would you? But Karin plates a dinner for Bianca to eat and makes her a bed that night. She creates a place at her table and a bed in her home. Karin gives Bianca clothes and Gus gets Bianca a wheelchair. When Bianca arrives at their doorstep, Gus and Karin don't know what to do next, but they know they can love Lars. When watching *Lars and the Real Girl* it's easier than you might imagine to forget that Bianca is a sex doll. All of Lars's friends do. That's the power of love. The strength of love completely overwhelms. It dominates and overthrows whatever else previously existed.

Love is something everyone already knows how to do. There are no new skills to learn and no training course. We all love every day. I know this because we all have someone in our lives whom we find easy to love. As the father of two daughters, not a day has passed when I have found either of them difficult to love. When they fail to follow directions, when they break glasses and plates (I think we only have four plates left in the entire house), when they come home with a discipline notice, when they underperform during an athletic event, and even talk back with sarcasm and cynicism, I've never found them difficult to love. I love them because I choose to. I may choose to because I have an innate sense of responsibility toward them or love them because we are biologically connected, but I still choose to. And I know it's a choice because there are fathers around the world who do not choose to love their children. Thousands of parents have experienced the greatest heartbreak at the hands of the fugitive impulses of their children. Children who have stolen money from them or have physically abused or abandoned them. Some parents have had children who cursed them and disappointed them beyond belief, yet they still love them. If love was predicated on people following the rules and living tidy lives, no child would be loved. Love has faintly little to do with the actions of the beloved. Love has everything to do with the choices of the loving.

The human capacity to love is our greatest strength when we choose it over our more contemptuous angels. We all choose to love someone for our own reasons. There are people in my life and yours who will never want for our love. There are no choices too grave or words too harsh they can visit on us that we would facilitate our rejection of their lives. Each offense against us and every time we are on the losing end of their misguided decisions is not enough for us to turn our backs on them. There are others for whom no redeeming act is adequate to gain our affections. But if we can extend unconditional love towards our children, spouses, parents, lifelong friends, and whoever else we might choose, then that ability is already warehoused within us. All that is left to do is to choose to redeploy those skills and export them to everyone in the world. Your most vehement enemy, the women and men we feel are most fiercely opposed to the way we think things ought to be, are loved by God and are intended, by God, to be loved by us. We each have the power within us to do the difficult things: love those that hate us. Forgive those that harm you. Encourage those who dismiss you. We already have the ability, we just have to want to.

The capacity to love and embrace others in the face of obstinacy, differences of opinion and lifestyle, political aggression, race, culture, economics, and all the other divisive hindrances of life is what defines Christianity. The beauty of our moment in history is that the Christian community doesn't need a particular person or party to get elected. We don't need a change in the tax code or to shout about social issues. We don't have to worry about the border or radical terrorists or ISIS or Iran. Nor do we need a disproportionate focus on the glitzy mechanics of church life, like bigger budgets, satellite campuses, better preaching, car giveaways, imitation rock concerts, and substituting Wally World for children's spiritual formation. While all those concerns are real and require prayer, thought, and work, the way to change the world is simple. Find someone to love. Go over and sit.

Bibliography

Acuna, Kirsten. "The Moment Nobel Peace Laureate Malala Yousafzai left Jon Stewart Speechless." Business Insider, February 10, 2015. http://www.businessinsider.com/malala-yousafzai-left-jon-stewart-speechless-2015-2.

Beck, Richard. *Unclean: Meditations on Purity, Hospitality, and Morality.* Eugene, OR: Cascade, 2011.

Bell, Rob. *Love Wins: A Book about Heaven, Hell, and the Fate of Every Person Who Ever Lived.* New York: HarperOne, 2011.

Black, Gary, Jr. *Preparing for Heaven: What Dallas Willard Taught Me about Living, Dying, and Eternal Life.* New York: HarperOne, 2015.

Frank, Robert H. "Why Luck Matters More than You Might Think." *The Atlantic,* May 2016. http://www.theatlantic.com/magazine/archive/2016/05/why-luck-matters-more-than-you-might-think/476394/.

Gladwell, Malcolm. *David and Goliath: Underdogs, Misfits, and the Art of Battling Giants.* New York: Little, Brown, 2013.

Gombis, Timothy G. *The Drama of Ephesians: Participating in the Triumph of God.* Downers Grove, IL; IVP Academic, 2010.

Gray, Fred D. *Bus Ride to Justice: Changing the System by the System; the Life and Works of Fred D. Gray, Preacher, Attorney, Politician.* Montgomery: Black Belt, 1995.

Jensen, David H. *In the Company of Others: A Dialogical Christology.* Cleveland: Pilgrim, 2001.

Jindal, Bobby. Fox News Iterview. February 9, 2015. http://video.foxnews.com/v/4041687062001/?playlist_id=2114913880001#sp=show-clips/primetime

Keegan, Marina. "The Opposite of Loneliness." *Yale Daily News,* May 27, 2012. http://yaledailynews.com/blog/2012/05/27/keegan-the-opposite-of-loneliness/.

King, Martin Luther, Jr. "Advice for Living." https://swap.stanford.edu/20141218225521/http://mlk-kpp01.stanford.edu/primarydocuments/Vol4/May-1958_AdviceForLiving.pdf.

Kirchick, James. "Squanderer in Chief." *LA Times.* April 28, 2009.

Lamott, Anne. *Traveling Mercies: Some Thoughts on Faith.* Waterville, ME: Thorndike, 1999.

Meacham, Jon. *American Gospel: God, the Founding Fathers and the Making of a Nation.* New York: Random House, 2007.

Mueller, John. *Overblown: How Politicians and the Terrorism Industry Inflate National Security Threats, and Why We Believe Them.* New York: Free, 2006.

Bibliography

Mueller, John, and Mark G. Stewart. *Chasing Ghosts: The Policing of Terrorism*. New York: Oxford University Press, 2016.

Nouwen, Henri. *In the Name of Jesus: Reflections on Christian Leadership*. New York: Crossroad, 1993.

Paulsell, William O. "Ways of Prayer: Designing a Personal Rule." *Weavings* 2.5 (November-December 1987).

Posner, Sarah. "Christians More Supportive of Torture than Non-religious Americans." *Religion Dispatches*, December 16, 2014. http://religiondispatches.org/christians-more-supportive-of-torture-than-non-religious-americans/.

Rohr, Richard. *Falling Upward: A Spirituality for the Two Halves of Life*. San Francisco: Jossey-Bass, 2011.

Scott, Eugene. "Trump Believes in God, but Hasn't Sought Forgiveness." *CNN*, July 18, 2015. http://www.cnn.com/2015/07/18/politics/trump-has-never-sought-forgiveness/.

Thompson, Derek. "Rich People Are Great at Spending Money to Make Their Kids Rich, Too." *The Atlantic*, April 7, 2015. http://www.theatlantic.com/business/archive/2015/04/being-rich-means-having-money-to-spend-on-being-richer/389871/.

Walsh, Brian J., and Sylvia Keemaat. *Colossians Remixed: Subverting the Empire*. Downers Grove, IL: InterVarsity, 2004.

Willard, Dallas. *The Great Omission: Reclaiming Jesus's Essential Teachings on Discipleship*. New York: HarperOne, 2014.

Wright, N. T. "Romans and the Theology of Paul." In vol. 3 of *Pauline Theology*, edited by David M. Hay and Elizabeth Johnson, 30–67. Minneapolis: Fortress, 1995.

Yancey, Philip. *Soul Survivor: How My Faith Survived the Church*. New York: Doubleday, 2001.

Made in the USA
Las Vegas, NV
24 January 2024

84830895R00114